MACMILLAN MOI

Macmillan Modern Dramatists
Series Editors: *Bruce King* and *Adele King*

Published titles

Reed Anderson, *Federico Garcia Lorca*
Eugene Benson, *J. M. Synge*
Renate Benson, *German Expressionist Drama*
Normand Berlin, *Eugene O'Neill*
Michael Billington, *Alan Ayckbourn*
John Bull, *New British Political Dramatists*
Denis Calandra, *New German Dramatists*
Neil Carson, *Arthur Miller*
Maurice Charney, *Joe Orton*
Ruby Cohn, *New American Dramatists, 1960–1980*
Bernard F. Dukore, *American Dramatists, 1918–1945*
Bernard F. Dukore, *Harold Pinter*
Arthur Ganz, *George Bernard Shaw*
Frances Gray, *John Arden*
Julian Hilton, *Georg Büchner*
David Hirst, *Edward Bond*
Helene Keyssar, *Feminist Theatre*
Bettina L. Knapp, *French Theatre 1918–1939*
Charles Lyons, *Samuel Beckett*
Susan Bassnett-McGuire, *Luigi Pirandello*
Margery Morgan, *August Strindberg*
Leonard C. Pronko, *Eugène Labiche and Georges Feydeau*
Jeanette L. Savona, *Jean Genet*
Claude Schumacher, *Alfred Jarry and Guillaume Apollinaire*
Laurence Senelick, *Anton Chekhov*
Theodore Shank, *American Alternative Theatre*
James Simmons, *Sean O'Casey*
David Thomas, *Henrik Ibsen*
Dennis Walder, *Athol Fugard*
Thomas R. Whittaker, *Tom Stoppard*
Nick Worrall, *Nikolai Gogol and Ivan Turgenev*
Katharine Worth, *Oscar Wilde*

Further titles in preparation

MACMILLAN MODERN DRAMATISTS

AUGUST STRINDBERG

Margery Morgan
Emeritus Reader in English,
University of Lancaster

MACMILLAN

First published 1985

Published by
Higher and Further Education Division
MACMILLAN PUBLISHERS LTD
Houndmills, Basingstoke, Hampshire RG21 2XS
and London
Companies and representatives
throughout the world

Typeset by
Wessex Typesetters Ltd
Frome, Somerset

Printed in Hong Kong

British Library Cataloguing in Publication Data
Morgan, Margery
August Strindberg.—(Macmillan modern dramatists)
1. Strindberg, August—Criticism and
interpretation
I. Title
839.7′26 PT9816
ISBN 0–333–29266–9
ISBN 0–333–29267–7 Pbk

Contents

	Editors' Preface	vi
	List of Plates	vii
	Acknowledgements	ix
1	Biographical: Fact and Fiction	1
2	Naturalistic Plays	21
3	Out of Inferno	40
4	In a Higher Court	54
5	Dramatist as Director	68
6	History Plays	90
7	*The Dance of Death*	111
8	Towards Total Theatre: *A Dream Play*	119
9	The Chamber Plays	132
10	Strindberg and the Theatre	147
	Appendix – Note on Frida Strindberg	171
	Notes and References	173
	Select Bibliography	180
	Index	188

Editors' Preface

The *Macmillan Modern Dramatists* is an international series of introductions to major and significant nineteenth and twentieth century dramatists, movements and new forms of drama in Europe, Great Britain, America and new nations such as Nigeria and Trinidad. Besides new studies of great and influential dramatists of the past, the series includes volumes on contemporary authors, recent trends in the theatre and on many dramatists, such as writers of farce, who have created theatre 'classics' while being neglected by literary criticism. The volumes in the series devoted to individual dramatists include a biography, a survey of the plays, and detailed analysis of the most significant plays, along with discussion, where relevant, of the political, social, historical and theatrical context. The authors of the volumes, who are involved with theatre as playwrights, directors, actors, teachers and critics, are concerned with the plays as theatre and discuss such matters as performance, character interpretation and staging, along with themes and contexts.

BRUCE KING

ADELE KING

List of Plates

1. August Strindberg with his daughters, Karin and Greta, in Switzerland, 1886. Pre-set exposure by Strindberg himself. (Strindberg Museum, Stockholm)
2. August Strindberg 'The City' painted between 1900 and 1907. (The National Museum, Stockholm)
3. Robert Loraine in *The Father*, directed by Milton Rosmer, Everyman and Apollo Theatres, London 1927.
4. Wilfred Lawson in *The Father*, directed by Peter Cotes, Arts Theatre, London 1953. (Photo: Angus McBean)
5. Beatrix Lehmann as Laura in *The Father*, Arts Theatre, London 1953. (Photo: Angus McBean)
6. *To Damascus*, directed by Ingmar Bergman, Royal Dramatic Theatre, Stockholm, 1974. Jan Olof Strindberg as The Unknown, right foreground. (Photo: Beata Bergström)
7. *Crimes and Crimes* (Broch och Brott) Royal Dramatic Theatre, Stockholm 1900. Augusta Lindberg as Henriette, August Palme as Maurice.

8. Harriet Bosse as Henriette, Uno Henning as Maurice, in *Crimes and Crimes*, directed by Alf Sjoberg, Royal Dramatic Theatre, Stockholm 1936.
9. *Charles XII/Karl XII* with August Palme as The King, RDT, Stockholm, 1902 (Nordiska Museum, Stockholm)
10. *Gustav Vasa*, Göteborg City Theatre 1934, directed by Kurt Ström, with Sven Miliander as Göran and Georg Rydeberg as Price Erik. (Museum of Theatre History, Göteborg)
11. *The Pelican* at Strindberg's Intimate Theatre, Stockholm, 1907–10. August Falck, as the Son, is on the left by the table, and Manda Bjorling, as the Daughter, is seated on the right. (Nordiska Museum)
12. The art nouveau design for *Swanwhite* at the Intimate Theatre. The set based on this was eventually abandoned and curtains were used instead. (Nordiska Museum)
13. Olof Molander's production of *Ghost Sonata*, at the Royal Dramatic Theatre, Stockholm, 1962. (Photo: Beata Bergström)
14. *A Dream Play*, produced by Victor Castegren, Svenska Theatre, Stockholm, 1907, with Harriet Bosse as Indra's Daughter. (Nordiska Museum)
15. Max von Sydow as The Stranger in Strindberg's *The Burned House* (Brända tomten), directed by Alf Sjöberg at the Royal Dramatic Theatre, Stockholm, 1970 (Photo: Beata Bergström)

Acknowledgements

I have accumulated indebtedness to many individuals and institutions, over years spent in pursuit of Strindberg, particularly in relation to productions of his plays. I have made acknowledgement to some of these elsewhere. Here I wish to add, or reiterate, thanks to: Peter Cotes and Joan Miller, Charles Marowitz, Michael Meyer, Anthony Swerling; The Traverse Theatre, the Swedish Institute, Stockholm, and Ingrid Mattson; Tom Olsson, librarian of the Royal Dramatic Theatre, Stockholm; the staff of the Strindberg Museum, Blå Tornet, and of the Drottningholm Theatre Museum, Kulturhuset, Stockholm; library staff and the photographic department of the Nordiska Museum, Stockholm; Åke Pettersson, Director of the Museum of Theatre History, Göteborg, and Britta Carlsson.

M.M.

Acknowledgements

The author and publishers wish to thank the following, who have kindly given permission for the use of copyright material:

Faber and Faber Ltd. for an extract from *The Family Reunion* (1939) by T. S. Eliot.

Martin Secker and Warburg Ltd. and David Higham Associates on behalf of Michael Meyer for extracts from *The Plays of Strindberg* (1964, 1975) by August Strindberg, translated by Michael Meyer.

For my daughter,
Siri

1
Biographical: Fact and Fiction

The years of August Strindberg's life, 1849–1912, fell within the most stable period of modern history. Born after the Year of Revolutions, he died two years before the start of the First World War. For much of his life he was a well-known public figure in his own country of Sweden, pilloried in middle age, and honoured on his sixtieth birthday by a torchlight procession of trade unionists and the presentation of an anti-Nobel prize, in popular protest at the neglect of the Swedish establishment to award him the official Nobel prize for literature.

The main challenges his time offered to artists and intellectuals came out of the struggle between religion and science, the questioning of the long-established order by emergent feminism, and a sense of repression leading towards sexual liberation. Though social equality remained a live issue, the pursuit of it generally took non-violent forms throughout Strindberg's lifetime. His work grapples with each of these concerns and from the end of the nineteenth century, while the power of the German military machine continued to grow, his anti-militarist and internationalist attitudes became more prominent. Yet his plays are not debating grounds for public questions. He is a dramatist of the mind, nerves and emotions, studying the internalisation of social forces within the psyche.

The Franco-Prussian war and the short-lived Paris Communc were already in the past when he made his first visit to France in 1876. For much of the 1880s and, again, for several years before the end of the century, he saw little of Sweden, living for the most part in the cosmopolitan, bohemian circles of Paris and Berlin, a recognised member of the artistic *avant-garde*, even when most reclusive. He was not exclusively involved in any one of the rival post-romantic movements in the arts. His international reputation was won with Antoine's presentation of *Miss Julie* at the Théâtre Libre in January 1893, followed by the production of *The Father* by Lugné-Poë's Théâtre de l'Oeuvre in December 1894.[1] The Preface Strindberg wrote for *Miss Julie*. and which Antoine distributed to the audience, identified the author with the extension of literary naturalism from prose fiction to drama. Emile Zola, the leading theorist of naturalism, had indeed adapted his own novel, *Thérèse Raquin*, for the stage; but Strindberg's two plays were undoubtedly the first masterpieces of the new movement in the theatre. The Théâtre Libre made naturalism in performance its principal concern; the Théâtre de l'Oeuvre, on the other hand, was particularly associated with the interpretation of Maurice Maeterlinck's symbolist plays. His association with each accurately reflects the way Strindberg's drama spans both fields. There was no conflict or contradiction, for him, in the practice of scientific experimentation and occult rituals and modes of thought; the contemporary intellectual life of Paris could and did hold them both.

His own view of his origins emphasised uncertainties of social position. As an autobiographical novelist, he was to fictionalise, rearrange and distort the facts of his life in ways that create peculiar difficulties for objective biographers. (Eugene O'Neill's autobiographical plays offer an instructive parallel.) From other sources we know that his father was a middle-class Stockholm merchant and his mother had been a servant.[2] August was their fourth child, born on 22 January 1849, sixteen months after their marriage. There were to be eleven children in the family, only seven surviving to adulthood. Their father went bankrupt in 1853, but made a financial recovery later. Undoubtedly, young August experienced shame and deprivation during his childhood, though possibly for shorter periods than the fictional accounts suggest. His relationship with his father was not close, and left him feeling unvalued.

His mother died when he was thirteen years old. A year later he acquired a stepmother, when his father married the housekeeper. Both women were pietists, fervent believers in a then-popular form of strict, evangelical Christianity, similar to methodism, and young August's spiritual life was profoundly influenced by this belief. Then, at the age of fifteen, he was drawn to the unitarianism of the American Theodore Parker. His religious development took a further turn with his excited reading of Ibsen's *Brand*, in 1869, and he followed this up with his first reading of Kierkegaard.

He had no clear and consistent idea of what career he should follow, only of the need to make money to live, which was to dog him for most of his life. In 1868 he worked as an elementary school teacher. He then went to Uppsala University to study medicine, but, on failing an examination, broke off his course, though he never lost interest in science and medicine. He tried to become an actor, entering the school of the Royal Dramatic Theatre* in Stockholm. Although this led to his first attempt at play-writing, it looked like a false move at the time in view of the small talent he showed for acting. He considered authorship as a profession after the publication of his first play, *The Freethinker*, and the performance of his one-act piece, *In Rome*, at Dramaten in 1870. However, he returned to Uppsala in the autumn, apparently to study for the new licentiate in philosophy, while also persisting in dramatic writing against his father's wishes. Adverse criticisms of his early plays, followed by the rejection of his first major play, *Master Olof*, by the Royal Dramatic Theatre, were serious discouragements; but the habit of living with a pen in his hand had become established. In 1872 he again left the university without a degree, made a further brief and unsuccessful attempt to become an actor in Göteborg, and then turned to journalism. This introduced him to the discussion of social and political questions which would be the basis of savagely satirical prose works written in the 1880s and, again, near the end of his life. He continued to try to alter *Master Olof* to meet the demands of the Royal Dramatic Theatre, producing a poetic version in 1876, which was received with no more favour than the first. Eventually, the New Theatre staged the play, in prose form, in 1881: this was Strindberg's first considerable theatrical success.

Meanwhile, he had been given an appointment in the Royal Library which led to his studying Chinese in order to catalogue the holdings in the Chinese section. For eight years from 1872 he worked happily at a profession, and in

---

* Sometimes referred to briefly as Dramaten, in these pages, just as Strindberg's Intimate Theatre may be called Intiman.

conditions, that suited him. The regularity of this life was disturbed by his meeting with Baron Carl Gustav Wrangel and his Finnish wife, Siri. Strindberg fell in love with the Baroness, who was restless in her marriage and ambitious for a career as an actress. The Wrangels' divorce was followed by Siri's marriage to Strindberg at the end of 1877. A daughter was born to them about a month later who died after two days. There were three other children of this marriage: Karin, born in 1880, Greta, born in 1881, and a son, Hans, born in 1884.

In 1879, Strindberg published his novel of bohemian café society, *The Red Room*, which made him generally known in Sweden. He followed this up by writing three plays: *The Secret of the Guild, Sir Bengt's Wife* and *Lucky Peter's Travels*. The second was written expressly for Siri, who had some success in the leading role in Stockholm in 1882, but was subsequently disappointed that her stage career did not develop. In the following year they left Sweden, missing the appreciative reception given to *Lucky Peter's Travels*, which ran for 76 performances; and they lived abroad until 1889 in France and Switzerland, visiting Italy, and spending further periods in Bavaria and Denmark. They had very little money, and Strindberg was seldom free of financial anxieties. At times he painted instead of writing, and thought of selling his paintings as a quicker way to make money than awaiting a return on books.

The heaviest blow in this period spent abroad followed the appearance in 1884 of his first collection of stories entitled *Giftas (Getting Married)*. This was brilliant, sophisticated work, cool and detached in its view of the varieties of sexual relationship within the social institution of marriage. Strindberg was attacking his society's repressive moralistic attitude to sex, and the related follies of romantic idealism. Taking the natural as his criterion of the healthy and good, his frankness only made his recommendations more offensive to contemporary 'purity' organisations approved by the Swedish Queen herself. He also tilted expressly, again and again, at 'the great jesuitical congregation which goes by the name of the upper class'. He had already made enemies by issuing a collection of satirical articles published under the title of *The New Kingdom* in 1882, and was apprehensive of trouble, though this did not make him muffle the challenge he was issuing. The only charge against *Getting Married* that would stick in a court of law proved to be one of blasphemy, based specifically on a sceptically mocking allusion to the bread and wine of the sacrament.[3] Strindberg went back to Stockholm from Switzerland for the trial and was acclaimed as a hero by the crowds who greeted his arrival and departure. Yet, in spite of this and the fact that he was technically acquitted, the whole experience distressed him greatly and convinced him that the powers in authority could deny him freedom of expression and even prevent him from earning a living by his pen.

Nevertheless, Strindberg issued a further collection of stories on sexual relationships as a second volume of *Getting Married*. These were more deeply sardonic than the first set, and sound a misogynist note more distinctly. Strindberg's jaundiced eye was not cast only on women. He was certainly moving towards atheism and scientific naturalism before the blasphemy trial, but these tendencies were confirmed after it and informed his fictionalised autobiography, *The Son of a Servant* (1886–7) and the group of plays which followed, including *Miss Julie* (1888).

Originally written in French, *Le Plaidoyer d'un Fou* (*A Madman's Defence*) (1888)[4] which belongs to the same period was the most notorious of all his books. It is a psychological case history whose basis on his marriage to Siri is thinly veiled. Whether Strindberg had realised in advance that his fictional devices of selection, arrangement and heightening would be generally discounted and the work taken to be a simple exposure of the marriage and the attitudes of the main participants is difficult to judge. He later described it as a 'terrible book' and expressed regret at having written it. In fact, his attitude to it was ambiguous. The prefaces he wrote for successive editions and his inclusion of the work in the plot of his play, *To Damascus*, as the unnamed book which the Lady is forbidden to read, indicate a realisation of the extent to which he had violated the ordinary sense of decent reticence about the intimacies of private life. That the book was originally intended to be daring is certain, as is the fact of its literary success, in which the author could take pride. It placed him in the vanguard of artistic experiment; but it also laid the foundations of public belief that he was mentally unbalanced as well as corrupt and corrupting. On the first publication of the book in German, Strindberg was again charged in a court of law, this time with 'indecency and immorality'.

The marriage to Siri was certainly going through a difficult period, yet it survived as a working partnership to the extent that Strindberg reverted to plans for a Scandinavian theatre, on the lines of Antoine's Théâtre Libre, which would be a showcase for his own plays and also give Siri an opportunity to employ her acting talents. At last, he made practical preparations for a season in Copenhagen, in 1889, even writing a number of short plays as new material for the repertoire. However, the Scandinavian Experimental Theatre closed very soon after it opened: after a moderately successful first week, *Miss Julie* was to be included in the programme – only to be banned by the authorities. The play was then performed semi-privately in a room at the University, but the death-blow had been given to the enterprise. The couple returned to Sweden (where Strindberg wrote his novel *By the Open Sea*) and the marriage broke up, ending in divorce in 1891. Although Strindberg married again twice, having a child by each of his later wives, only this first marriage lasted for any considerable time.

His second wife, Frida Uhl, was the daughter of a well-known Austrian newspaper editor and herself a cosmopolitan 'new woman'. They met in Berlin in 1892, the year of the German première of *Miss Julie.* No doubt Frida was attracted to the great author as well as to the tall man with striking looks. It was her determination to help his career that brought them to England, where she could act as his interpreter and compensate for his diffidence with her advocacy. Despite his growing fame, he was virtually destitute at this time, and in this condition, the pair went to visit her grandparents in Austria. Strangely enough, Frida herself seems to have had less effect on Strindberg's development as a writer than her family. Her mother was instrumental in bringing the teachings of Swedenborg seriously to his attention during the period of emotional disturbance commonly referred to as his 'Inferno crisis', the breakdown which coincided with and supplied the subject for the novel, *Inferno* (1897). The couple were apart more than they were together while the legal marriage lasted, but even while their divorce was being arranged, August stayed with his wife's family at Dornach (in Austria), ostensibly visiting his little daughter Kerstin (born in 1894) while Frida herself was in Paris and Berlin, and, unknown to her husband, became pregnant by Frank Wedekind. He still hoped for a resumption of the relationship with Frida, but to no avail, though she continued to call herself Madame

Strindberg throughout her subsequent career. (See pp. 171–2 below.)

During his second marriage, which ended in 1897, Strindberg abandoned all literary work for other pursuits, particularly scientific investigations. He had written a collection of *Little Studies of Plants and Animals* in 1888. Back in Paris, in 1895, he devoted himself increasingly to chemistry. As well as being a resumption of earlier interests, the change of occupation emulated Goethe and Swedenborg, whose studies were as universal as Leonardo's in their scope. He never withdrew for long from the artists' colony, and was better known than before as a man-of-letters following the theatrical success of *The Father* (1887), presented by Lugné-Poë in 1894. W. B. Yeats met him, and Frederick Delius, the composer, later published his recollections of Strindberg, experimenting with sulphur and carbon and embarking on the old alchemical quest to prove that base metals could be turned into gold.[5] In this late-nineteenth-century guise, it was a logical part of Strindberg's Darwinian programme to establish the basic unity and relatedness of all forms of life. The superficially similar doctrine of correspondences, within the aesthetic of Symbolism, was a resumption of mediaeval belief. For Strindberg, as perhaps for others in that period of the revival of 'alternative' traditions, the two theories seem increasingly to have coalesced. Occultism was flourishing in Paris, and Strindberg contributed his observations regularly to the leading occultist journal, *L'Initiation*.

Since the mid-twentieth century Strindberg has aroused interest as a modernist painter, and some of his surviving pictures are records of the time he spent in Austria. He continued painting after his return to Paris in 1894. During his marriage to Siri he had known Paul Gauguin, who now asked his Swedish friend to write an introduction to the catalogue for his exhibition intended to raise money for a return to the South Seas. It was an appeal to a successful playwright whose sympathies were with revolutionary movements in the arts. Gauguin published Strindberg's reply, with its reservations, as his Introduction, and indeed it seems likely that this is what Strindberg intended. This was also the period when Strindberg's influence became most apparent in the work of another friend, the Norwegian painter, Edvard Munch.[6]

Strindberg and Munch had both been erotically fascinated by, and involved with, the remarkable Dagny Juel (familiar to us as the model for the *femme fatale* in some of Munch's pictures), in Berlin before August's marriage to Frida. He may, indeed, have been Dagny's lover while engaged to Frida; certainly he felt guilty because of the sexual attraction this woman held for him and regarded her as a dangerous creature. She married one of the Zum Schwarzen Ferkel group, the Pole, Stanislas Przybyszewski, who figures largely in Strindberg's fantasies in the next few years – as his principal persecutor and would-be murderer. When news came to him of the death of Przybyszewski's common-law wife (she killed herself when he had abandoned her for Dagny), this became the basis of his identification of the Pole as the murderer of his wife and children, in which Strindberg may have been projecting his own guilt at the poverty of Siri and their children at this time, when he was contributing nothing to their support. As in 1892 a collection made by Ola Hansson had enabled Strindberg to go from Stockholm to Berlin. From October 1894 until the summer of 1896, only money found for him by friends and admirers saved him from starvation: experiences represented in his later drama through the symbolic character of the Beggar.

His desperate and persistent financial difficulties were enough in themselves to make some form of breakdown likely, and the loneliness he suffered after separating from Frida in 1894 also played its part, though these factors do not entirely account for the psychotic disorders from which he suffered at intervals until 1897. This was not merely a case of sickness, it was also a process of spiritual adventuring, a kind of pilgrimage through modes of experience valued in the intellectual and artistic circles of contemporary Paris. Strindberg was not the only fin-de-siècle artist to court self-destruction in the pursuit of worlds beyond the limitations of commonsense and one-dimensional reason. (Rimbaud's *Season in Hell* offers a general parallel.) In the essay he wrote on 'Deranged Sensations' and published in instalments late in 1894 and early in 1895, Strindberg declared, 'Disorder reigns in my universe, and that is freedom'.[7] It is a manifesto of neo-romanticism and of the protean quality of imagination.

The damage caused to the skin of Strindberg's hands by his scientific experiments led to treatment at the Hôpital Saint-Louis, in spring, 1895. As his obsessions and hallucinations continued, and in alarm that he might really be losing his sanity, he fled back to Sweden in 1896 and put himself under the care of Dr Eliasson of Ystad for some months. After another visit to Austria and a return to Paris in 1897, when he was nearest conversion to Catholicism, being back in his native land contributed to the healing process. However eccentric and neurotic he might be in the rest of his life, the psychotic states did not recur. He started to write again; and Strindberg the author was a sane man.

Indeed, the years immediately after his emergence from

'Inferno' were splendidly creative: the inferno experiences proved a rich mine for numerous works differing markedly from anything he had previously written. Most of the dramatic and theatrical experiments of the twentieth century were anticipated by Strindberg now; and it is to these 'post-Inferno' dramas that so many later master-playwrights and directors became indebted.

It was through the casting of a young Norwegian actress called Harriet Bosse as Indra's Daughter, in *A Dream Play* (1901), and the Lady, in *To Damascus* (1898–1901), that Strindberg discovered his third wife – a considerably more accomplished actress than Siri had been. Their marriage took place in 1901. Setting aside the disparity between their ages, there were undoubtedly sympathies between Harriet and Strindberg. His jealousy – not so unusual in the so-much-older husband of a rising actress – and a new and timid reluctance to forsake his domestic routine and the environs of his Stockholm home, even for a holiday, made it difficult for Harriet to continue living with him, but she visited him frequently, dining with him, and sometimes they slept together, for more than two years after the divorce of 1904. When she remarried, Harriet had some difficulty in persuading Strindberg that he must stop writing to her and thinking of her as his wife; and many entries in what he had started as an occult diary (after the model of Swedenborg's) touchingly record the erotic fantasies in which he persuaded himself that her spirit was seeking his in sexual love. These sensations graduated into pain which he eventually realised was organic: it was symptomatic of the cancer which was to kill him in 1912.

Meanwhile, a long-desired goal was reached when the young actor-manager, August Falck, approached him with proposals for starting a Strindberg theatre in Stockholm. For five years Strindberg's thoughts were constantly occupied with plans for the tiny Intima Theatre, its repertoire, rehearsals, problems of staging. In a last great outburst of playwriting he composed five new plays specifically for this theatrical enterprise. The presentation of a considerable portion of his *oeuvre* – from all periods and in a range of dramatic styles and moods – established his status as one of the greatest dramatists, a world figure. At last, and before the anti-Nobel prize was presented to him, his work was bringing in royalties, his financial situation was secure and he could live in the comfortable and elegant style that appealed to him, though the domestic arrangements were rarely close enough to perfection to quieten his critical irritability. His apartment was the setting of weekly evenings of music-making by the same small group of friends, including his brother. He was on good terms with his children and took particular pleasure in the visits of his youngest, Harriet's daughter, Anne-Marie. The Indian summer of his life revived old hopes in him: he developed an emotional interest in the young dancer, Fanny Falkner, who played small parts at the Intima Theatre and to whom he gave the lead in *Swanwhite*. He moved to an apartment in the house where her family lived (the Blue Tower which now houses the Strindberg Museum) and persuaded her to become engaged to him. When she broke off the engagement, he took his disappointment quietly: and then, when his experimental theatre had closed, his vitality flared up in a number of polemical prose writings that brought him back into the centre of Sweden's national and political life. He died on 14 May 1912, when the first Anglo-American collected edition of his plays in translation was already well advanced.

The last of his autobiographical novels, written in 1903, was called *Ensam* (*Alone*). For much of his life, Strindberg suffered from loneliness partly determined by his own shyness, which it also intensified. To be much alone is an inevitable fate of the professional writer; and Strindberg had come to accept this condition of the creative activity in which he lived most fully and with the deepest joy.

No survey of Strindberg's life can ignore the range of his non-dramatic prose fiction, the extent to which he wrote up that life as fiction and the close imaginative relationship between his autobiographical novels in particular and his plays. *The Red Room* published in 1879 (and not to be confused with the similarly titled *In the Red Room*, or *In the Rose Room*, third part of *The Son of a Servant*) was Strindberg's first public success: a generally lighthearted novel of social observation. In focussing on a group of friends and acquaintances who frequent the café which gave the book its title, Strindberg found an adaptable form which interposed only a slight barrier between his fiction and the actuality of Stockholm life; the genre is essentially that of *The Pickwick Papers*. He returned to the same general formula in *The Gothic Rooms* of 1904; and the original form of 'The Quarantine Master's Second Story',[8] dealing with the period of his second marriage, was entitled *The Cloister*, referring both to the Belgian monastery where he spent 24 hours and to the Berlin café, which Strindberg called Zum Schwarzen Ferkel (the Black Pig). This kind of double relevance, sometimes going as far as allegory, is characteristic of most of Strindberg's work.

His best-liked novel is *The People of Hemsö* (*Hemsöborna*, 1887) which seems little burdened by ulterior meanings, but is coloured and enlivened by love of his native land and interest in traditional ways of life and regional characteristics. It is the kind of study into the relationship between climate, topography and culture, advocated by Auguste Taine and practised by Pierre Loti in

Pêcheur d'Islande (1886) and in J. M. Synge's peasant plays. A shrewd interloper, the unscrupulous Carlsson, takes on a peasant community, building up his fortunes through gaining dominance over the rest and organising their lives. He is ultimately defeated by the elements and the sheer persistence of the rhythms of peasant life. Strindberg's detachment and equal appreciation of the qualities of each side preserve the balance of comedy, despite Carlsson's fate.

I Havsbandet (1890), translated under the alternative titles, *By the Open Sea* and *In the Outer Skerries*, is a metaphysical counterpart of *Hemsöborna*, though more obviously challenging in its technique and disturbing in its subject matter. Modelled in a general way on Victor Hugo's *Toilers of the Sea*, it presents a distinctively Nietzschean hero, a scientist, a 'superior' being whose social and geographical isolation mirrors the isolation of his intellect and will and more finely tuned sensibility from the humanity of mankind in general. This powerful novel was close to the philosophical mainstream of new and serious art of its time. It traces the destruction, breakdown through madness and then annihilation by the sea itself, of the man who pursues an extreme. The hubris suggests an ancient tragic pattern which also haunts some of Joseph Conrad's work, reminiscent, for example, of the character and situation of Axel Heyst, in *Victory*. The solitary voyage of Strindberg's Axel Borg, seeking his death in the infinite depths, is strikingly paralleled in Martin Decoud's aimless drifting in a small boat to his death 'from loneliness and loss of faith' in Conrad's *Nostromo*.

The influence of Nietzsche, and the idea of the 'battle of brains'[9] which informs the plot of several of Strindberg's naturalistic plays, is also evident in *Tschandala* (1888)[10] (written between *Hemsöborna* and *I Havsbandet*), one of the simplest examples of how Strindberg used his own experiences as the basis of fiction. The events of this book correspond to incidents in which Strindberg was involved when he, Siri and the children were staying as paying guests on an estate north of Copenhagen; but *Tschandala* transposes the situation and characters to the eighteenth century, as well as changing names and identities (highlighting his opponent's possible gipsy origins, changing half-sister to daughter and turning his own substitute into a university professor). The locale is made to seem eerie, unrealistic. Confused and inconclusive happenings are transformed into a regular, constructed plot, and the story has a sensational invented climax in which the hero's scientific knowledge enables him to play on the gipsy's superstitious fears by creating a sham marvel, a contrived 'magical' effect. So *Tschandala* demonstrates the defeat of the primitive by the man of intellect (a contrast to the outcome of the 'battle of brains' in *The Father*). Strindberg certainly fantasised incidents in which he had really played a fairly ignominious role, yet if its origins were unknown, the book would be completely acceptable as a psychological thriller. The psychological understanding on which the work is based rests on a knowledge of Maudsley's *Pathology of Mind* and Nietzsche's theory of the master-slave relationship from *The Genealogy of Morals*.

Strindberg had begun organising the events of his own life into a multi-volumed work before writing either of his island novels. The general scheme he followed was that of the *Bildungsroman*, tracing the emergence of the author through the experiences of childhood, adolescence and early maturity. *The Author* is, in fact, the title of the fourth book of the series, following *The Son of a Servant* (1886), *Time of Ferment* (also 1886) and *In the Red Room*, written during 1887. The first of these introduced a subtitle for the whole projected undertaking: 'The Growth of a Soul'. This way of writing up his experiences became habitual and was doubtless therapeutic, so that he eventually left a wide scattering of volumes and tales which reflect different phases of his life but do not fit together perfectly as parts of a single structure. The recent critical swing from reading these works simply as autobiography, sometimes inaccurate, sometimes deliberately distorted, to reading them as a particular kind of novel, most familiar to English readers in the example of James Joyce's *Portrait of the Artist as a Young Man*, has a startling result: the works themselves seem to undergo an actual change of nature, show new qualities and become interesting in new ways. This has consequences for the interpretation of his plays, though none of them – because of the obvious artifice of the form – was ever quite so mistakable as simple autobiographical fact.

From *The Author* Strindberg proceeded to *Le Plaidoyer d'un Fou* (*A Madman's Defence*), written in French, and not published in a Swedish version (by J. Landquist) until 1914. It was based on the gradual breakdown of his marriage with Siri; he stressed the authenticity of the material and originally wanted to include with the narrative the love letters that had passed between them. (Eventually, these were published separately under the title, *He and She*, in 1919.[11]) Jealousy and suspicion are the chief themes of the book, perfectly matched by the presentation of situation, incident and character entirely as they appear to the central character in the enclosed world of his mind. Strindberg calls the focal character Johan, without giving him a surname. Johan is also the name of the hero of *The Son of a Servant* whose experiences are narrated in that book by a third-person commentator. Johan was, of course, Strindberg's own first name, but not the name he generally used and was known by. Strindberg was certainly creating a hybrid form: linking the third-person method of narration, which seems to guarantee objectivity, to a concentration on the mental processes of an alter ego, who is arguably the only character in the book. He spoke of his aim in writing *Inferno* also in French (1897) in terms of becoming a 'Zola of the occult'. This implies an extension of naturalism.

Emile Zola had theorised about the naturalistic novelist as a scientific experimenter – not just an observer and analyst – concerned with a form of truth he scarcely distinguished from sociological fact. Strindberg's experiments involved bringing his art dangerously close to actual life, challenging the conventions of aesthetic distance and the usual pretence that the author is quite outside the novel (or play), godlike in his detachment. His autobiographical novels test what happens to fiction when such conventions are set aside and, simultaneously, challenge the claim of factual truth to absoluteness and neutrality. Perhaps it is in this light that we should read his often-quoted remark about *The Father*, that he did not know if it was 'something I have imagined or if my life was really like this'. It may be that only a fanatical artist would raise the question, whether imaginative insight is something new and additional, extrapolated from experience, or whether it is a perception of the deep truth of that experience which commonsense fails to recognise. From the point of view of normality and commonsense we may suspect that the accounts we are given in *A Madman's Defence* and *Inferno* are biased and distorted. On the books' own terms, the concepts of normality and distortion are themselves called into question. The comment of G. Brandell, student of Strindberg's chief emotional crises, is worth pondering: 'There is nothing, so far as I know, to indicate that the suspicions he voices in *A Madman's Defence* survived the composition of the work'.[12] It can lead to the question of whether Strindberg's procedure in writing that book was very different from the usual activity of the novelist who imaginatively extrapolates the emotional substance of his work from his own inner life, including giving rein to doubts and fears, fancies and speculations, which he would not readily identify as the objective truth of his experience in the world.

E. O. Johannesson has interestingly suggested an analogy between *A Madman's Defence* and such exemplars of the novel of consciousness as F. M. Ford's *The Good Soldier* and Henry James's *The Turn of the Screw*, in which the narrator uncovers and presents 'the truth' of a situation but becomes an increasingly questionable medium of interpretation and, ultimately, the focal character in the work, to be judged as other characters are judged.[13] We know that in the late 1880s, Strindberg became passionately interested in Edgar Allan Poe, pioneer explorer of subjective states and the kind of occult experience presented in *Inferno*, through the hero's consciousness of unseen forces and, especially, a personal malignancy directing his life from a distance. His detailed, objective presentation of a character tormented by his superstitious, obsessive and symbol-making tendencies depends on self-knowledge and on artistic control. As a work of fiction, *Inferno* is comparable with Guy de Maupassant's tour-de-force, *Le Horla*. Eugene O'Neill deliberately followed Strindberg's example in some of his plays, including *Long Day's Journey into Night*, in turning his own life (and his family's) into the story-material of his art with minimal disguise. In prose fiction, Franz Kafka is Strindberg's chief disciple as chronicler and explorer of a disorientated subjectivity.

Inferno is the novel most closely linked with Strindberg's plays, sharing much of its material, and the view of life as a spiritual journey implied in its title, with Parts I and II of *To Damascus*. Together, these works mark his return to writing after the break of 1895–7, his crisis years. The hero of *Inferno* is, like Borg of *By the Open Sea*, a scientist, not a man of letters; but then he and the Unknown in *To Damascus* are given a mythic identification with Faust. Not that this is the only parallel figure Strindberg associates with them: the treatment of his own life as the stuff of myth, unstable in form and of multiple aspects, is one of the most striking characteristics of this phase of his career, marking a shift back to a religious sense of life.

All Strindberg's novels share the primacy of psychological analysis over narrative plot; his own *personae* are the subjects of literary case-histories. The large number of short stories he wrote, apart from the *Getting Married* collection – a collection of objective histories – is far too varied to permit generalisation. It may be easier to credit the humour of the 'gloomy Swede', which intrudes so often into his accounts of torment, if we recollect the enthusiasm for American humorous writers, including Mark Twain, which led to his translating and anthologising extracts from their work.[14]

2
Naturalistic Plays

It was as a naturalistic playwright that Strindberg first established his theatrical reputation outside Sweden. His first work in naturalistic vein was *Marauders*, revised and given the new title *Comrades* (completed in 1887). There followed in order: *The Father* (1887), *Miss Julie* and *Creditors* (1888), and a number of *quart d'heure* plays, *The Stronger, Pariah* and *Simoon* (1888–9). In 1892, he wrote further plays in the same general style. The one-act *Playing with Fire* is most frequently produced today. *The Bond*, a play about divorce proceedings which requires bit-players for a full jury, is perhaps the most impressive. *The First Warning, Debit and Credit, Facing Death*, and *Mother Love* share material and themes with more important plays, earlier and later in the chronology of his drama. As the author of *The Father* and *Miss Julie*, Strindberg would rank among the most important playwrights of the modern age, even if he had written nothing else for the theatre after 1892. Indeed he made a different reputation with his later work, and this has sometimes led to the retrospective assessment of the finest of the earlier plays as much less naturalistic than their author claimed.

Setting aside the confusion between the narrower application of the term 'naturalism' to an artistic method, a surface realism often symbolised by the camera eye, and what Strindberg terms 'the greater naturalism', a philosophic approach embracing the scientific attitude, it can fairly be said that this main body of his earlier drama was all written from the viewpoint of a freethinker, regarding all events and experiences as explicable, however complex and obscure their causal origins might be. Awareness of scientific concepts of the late nineteenth century is demonstrated in all the plays. Strindberg had been a medical student, and his characters live as much in a world of blood transfusion as of electricity and the telegraph. He links their behaviour with physiological conditions and afflictions of the nervous system – anaemia, epilepsy, hysteria – as well as with physical and mental heredity and the environmental factors, with which a developing social science was concerned. *Simoon*, once the most praised of his *quart d'heure* pieces, now seems the stagiest, a sham-exotic playlet of the revenge of an Arab girl on her faithless lover; but it is typical of the whole group in its presentation of the power of suggestion, in the deliberate exercise of one will over another, much studied in the psychology of the day. The techniques of the hypnotist are employed by Gustav in *Creditors*; the Nurse in *The Father* makes naïve use of the power of suggestion to get the Captain into a straitjacket. Theatrical entertainments which exploited hypnotism as a form of stage magic are acknowledged in the dialogue to be the model for the brilliant and horrifying ending of *Miss Julie*.

Strindberg's naturalism may have been more selective than he admitted, as it focussed on aspects of the new science which lent themselves to spectacular and intense dramatic action. His work of the 1880s is as much a meeting place of scientific ideas and the romantic imagination as R. L. Stevenson's *Dr Jekyll and Mr Hyde*. With the advance of scientific knowledge and the revision of scientific theories, present-day audiences and readers are probably more aware of the romantic and sensational aspects: the mysteriousness of the occult rather than the experimental spirit in occult practices. Yet, in *The Father*, Strindberg puts superstition in its place as an expression of the ignorance of his women characters (their power most eerily suggested by the witch-like spiritualist grandmother kept off-stage except for a single call which establishes her actuality) who beset the Captain, an enlightened man of science with no belief in God. When he shows Julie trying to creep into the shelter of her cook's pietism, it is a sign of the abject weakness to which the character is reduced. Gustav, in *Creditors*, draws a conclusion acceptable to the sophisticated society in which he and the other characters of the play belong:

> To a certain degree we cannot be blamed. But there is a margin of choice . . . We are innocent, but responsible; innocent in the eyes of God – but he no longer exists – yet responsible to ourselves and our fellow-beings.
>
> (trans. M. Meyer, I, 218)

His words recall the free-thinking Rebecca West in Ibsen's *Rosmersholm*, who has drawn the Pastor over to her own rational, irreligious understanding of morality: 'There is no judge over us. We must be our own judges'.

This Ibsen play prompted Strindberg to write the essay 'On Psychic Murder'[1] which offers a rationale for the idea on which the plots of his own naturalistic plays were based. What has proved more lastingly valuable in these plays is their exposure of how actions and relationships are governed by the individual's subjective reading of the external world. This is a form of poetic imagination, a human fact, fit material for investigation; and the same may be said of the religious beliefs of the characters – another particular concern of Strindberg – their way of explaining their experience of the world to themselves. The scientific study of religions by anthropologists and comparative religionists was a major element in late-nineteenth-century intellectual progress. The word 'myth' came into general use at this time, carrying the implication that religions do not rest on facts but on traditional stories and iconographies, part of the shared consciousness of a community.

His departures from a simply naturalistic dialogue are a sign that Strindberg was unwilling to be confined to the commonsense view of the world and impatient of keeping at all times to a style not always adequate to the further reaches of his purpose. However, the passages of naturalistic speech, up-to-date, racy and flexible, are among the strengths of his plays. This style establishes the characters of *The Father* as comprehensible, familiar to the audience, in Act I, before nightmare takes over and calls usual values and assumptions into question:

> CAPTAIN: Well, why didn't you lay into him? . . . you just sat there mumbling to yourself. . . .
> PASTOR: You've too many women running your home.
> CAPTAIN: You needn't tell me that. It's like a cage full of tigers – if I didn't keep a red-hot iron [under] their noses, they'd claw me to the ground the first chance they got. Yes, you can laugh, you old fox! It wasn't enough that I married your sister, you had to palm your old stepmother off on me too.
>
> (trans. M. Meyer, I 34–5)

The Captain evidently has a turn for metaphor, but uses it lightly and humorously. He has learnt to compromise and make the best of things, and the tone of his remarks is kept to the level of realistic tolerance:

> CAPTAIN: My dear brother-in-law, will you kindly tell me how one keeps women in their place?
> PASTOR: To speak frankly, Laura – I know she's my sister, but – well, she was always a little difficult.
> CAPTAIN: Oh, Laura has her moods, but she's not too bad.
> PASTOR: Ah! come on! I know her!
> CAPTAIN: Well, she's had a romantic upbringing, and has a little difficulty in accepting life . . .
>
> (trans. M. Meyer)

Ibsen's *Ghosts* was a recent model for a scientifically naturalistic drama in a middle-class domestic setting, but had also taken the ancient imagery of spiritual forces, such as the Fates and the Eumenides, translating it rationally into an awareness of natural and social forces that trap the individual in a tragic *impasse*. Strindberg's hero, in *The Father*, names Mrs Alving, the central figure of *Ghosts*, and so supplies the immediate cultural context for his own tragedy. Both authors were harking back to Greek tragedy, wanting to create a modern drama with comparable qualities of intensity and sublimity lacking in the most serious of recent dramatic forms, the well-made play.

His *Open Letters to the Intimate Theatre* testify that Strindberg deliberately studied play construction. Indeed it would have been foolish to ignore 'construction' in the heyday of the well-made play. Though the Preface to *Miss Julie* specifically rejects 'the symmetrical, mathematically constructed dialogue . . . favoured in France', Strindberg, like Ibsen, certainly did not jettison the entire classical tradition of play-writing. *The Father* is a three-act play which traces a single, inexorable dramatic action, keeps to a single domestic setting, concentrates increasingly on a single figure, treated heroically, and by clever trickery compresses the chain of events into a virtually unbroken continuity closely matching the duration of the performance. Without any equivalent for the choric odes of Greek tragedy to give pause for reflection, the sweep of passion, after the first scene, is all the more precipitate. The notion Strindberg was to express in the Preface to *Miss Julie*, that modern audiences had lost the capacity to give themselves up to illusion, justifies this dramatic rhythm.

With Act III, the play moves decisively into a mythic action. From the start the Captain, by virtue of his profession, has figured as a representative of the traditional warrior male. In personality he is no more military than the Count (unseen but described biographically) in *Miss Julie* is commanding and tyrannical; in each case, Strindberg shows us the gap between the actuality and the archetype. Now, when the mind of the protagonist takes over more completely as the field of the drama, that gap is narrowed almost to the point of extinction. Adolf has been established as a man of science too. It is his culture, his reading in world literature, that dictates the form of his obsession: as he finds in his books previously unnoticed testimony to the superior strength of women whose child-bearing gives them a hold on actuality and rescues them from the shadows of doubt and uncertainty which are the inevitable lot of the man. The father reads his personal fate as part of a general overthrow of male power by the alternative power of the weak: the wily and treacherous power of the serpent by which alone women can gain their ends. Such is the myth – compound of such prophetic legends as those of Hercules submissive to Omphale, or Samson in the hands of Delilah

– which Adolf reconstructs to fill the vacuum left by the departed image of God the Father. To the Nurse, who does not understand, he quotes from the 'Magnificat', that anthem of revolution which hails the emergent power (of those who have been weak) in the elevation of the chosen woman, Mary. With an ambiguous touch, the playwright makes the priest seem to endorse the triumph of Laura, the new order, at the end of the play, with an 'Amen!' which may more logically follow from the Doctor's words:

> DOCTOR: We must not judge or accuse him. You, who believe that there is a God who rules men's destinies, must plead this man's cause before the bar of Heaven.
> NURSE: Oh, Pastor, he prayed to God in his last moment!
> . . .
> DOCTOR: Then my art is useless. Now you must try yours, Pastor. . . . My knowledge ends here. He who knows more, let him speak.
> BERTHA (*enters left and runs to her mother*): Mother, mother!
> LAURA: My child! *My* child!
> PASTOR: Amen!
>
> (trans. M. Meyer, I, 87)

This distinctly ritualistic close suggests the death of Adolf, as of male domination. In fact, he has suffered a stroke from which he seems unlikely to recover. The end of *The Father* is thus at once final and suggestive of another time scale, a larger range of action, in which this is the ending of a single movement in a continuous, perhaps cyclical rhythm such as Strindberg's later plays present. (*The Father* is set in stormy December, at the winter solstice.) The fact that he went on to write *Miss Julie* indicates that Strindberg did not see the process of social change in his own day as moving uninterruptedly and altogether in one direction.

Strindberg begins to increase the length of the Captain's speeches in the course of Act II. Soon the brief comments of others hardly serve to check or divert the torrent. Having set events in train, even Laura joins the spectators of the drama within the single consciousness – to which the traditional tragic dialogue-conventions of tirade and soliloquy are entirely apt. 'You know', says Laura, shortly before the end of Act II, 'you ought to have been a poet'; and the greater freedom of expression Strindberg allows Adolf, the more trapped he becomes, and the play is turned into an essentially poetic drama. But it is still the kind of poetry he wrote in non-dramatic form: as rich in satire as in romantic lyricism of melancholy, nostalgia, terror and despair.[2]

In talking to Bertha, the Captain tries to explain in terms of such fantastic images as children know from folk tales, and there is a strong self-irony in his speech:

> BERTHA: . . . I want to be myself!
>
> CAPTAIN: You mustn't do that! You see, I'm a cannibal, and I want to eat you. Your mother wanted to eat me, but she couldn't. I am Saturn, who ate his children because it had been prophesied that otherwise they would eat him. To eat or be eaten! That is the question . . . But don't be afraid, my beloved child. I won't hurt you. (*Goes to where the guns are on the wall and takes a revolver.*)
>
> (trans. M. Meyer, I, 81–2)

This drawing on classical myth, as well as on the tones and grotesque images of the Elizabethan malcontent, here Hamlet specifically, absorbs even what may at first have seemed a directly naturalistic psychology of sex: as in the man's divided image of woman as mother and whore, his love and trust of the one and his fear of the other. In this, too, Strindberg has taken a prevailing contemporary theme, also evident in his friend Edvard Munch's paintings; but, between Adolf and Laura, it turns into the incest theme that haunts Greek tragedy and gave Freud a name for the Œdipus complex. (Similarly, in *Miss Julie*, the imagery of the dreadful banquet of Chronos links with the menstruating woman's obsession with blood to make Julie's pent-up fear and hatred of men voice itself hysterically in a fantasy of the dismemberment of the male and engorgement with his blood.)

Unlike Ibsen's *A Doll's House*, *The Father* does not indicate any possible reform of the social roles of men and women which would revolutionise marriage and bring the reality nearer to the idea. Strindberg de-romanticises marriage, exposing it as it seems to the eyes of the naturalist from which the scales have fallen: as a lifelong bondage which, given the evolutionary law of strife – one ego jostling the other constantly for the advantage – can only produce suffering and exhaustion. Laura's actions are very reasonably motivated by her discovery of where she stands in the eyes of the law (as a married woman and a mother, she has 'sold her birthright by legal contract' and cannot challenge her husband's decisions about the upbringing of their child), and she rebels against the consequence, that her daughter will come to believe 'that everything I taught her is nonsense', and fears 'she'll despise her mother for the rest of her life'. Discovery of the law shows her how she can escape from her situation: if her husband is declared insane, his authority can be vested in her. Seeing how law rests on fictions and unproven assumptions, it is by attacking these that she is able to upset her husband's mental balance. As Strindberg indicates, at the end, the destruction of the male is an incidental consequence of Laura's instinct to fight against her virtual annihilation as a human being. The play is more impartial in its view of marriage than are productions in which Laura is played as a monster; what they respond to is Strindberg's choice of emotional intensity as the key effect of his play, in place of the logical analysis Ibsen had brought to the same topic. If it were a factitious emotionalism, an inflated stage effect, *The Father* could be dismissed simply as melodrama; on the contrary, its emotional power is testimony to the irrational strength of feeling on which social institutions and customs rest.

Strindberg's Preface to *Miss Julie* is possibly the most famous manifesto of naturalism, and nothing in it is better known than his insistence on a solid, realistic kitchen set, instead of the bad old habit of painting shelves, pots and pans on canvas. It has not always been observed that the movement towards realistic staging had started thirty to forty years earlier. In England, Henry Irving was the innovator who plunged the auditorium into darkness in order to strengthen the grip of dramatic illusion on the audience ('if we could have . . . complete darkness in the auditorium during the performance . . . perhaps a new drama might emerge', wrote Strindberg). The Preface nods towards Antoine's innovations in performance ('I do not dream that I shall ever see the full back of an actor throughout the whole of an important scene'),[3] which supported the convention of the stage as a room with the fourth wall removed and such insulation of the play from the audience as was to culminate in the television screen. In general, however, Strindberg's more technical recommendations (e.g., abolition of footlights and heavy make-up; unbroken performance) are related to the conditions of intimate theatre rather than to naturalism as it has come to be understood in Britain: the surface realism which, by minimising the distinction between art and life, suppresses emotional disturbance and critical questioning.

He was soon pouring scorn on the fuss he had made over conventionalised staging and a doctrinaire meticulousness in naturalistic method: 'If a woman is seduced in a hothouse, it isn't necessary to relate the seduction to all the potted plants you can find there and list them all by name' (an allusion to his listing of the multiple conditions which motivate Julie's tragedy with the complexity of motivation we recognise in actual life). His 1889 essay, 'On Modern Drama and Modern Theatre',[4] keeps only to the philosophic core, where science and the traditional dynamics of drama meet: 'The great naturalism . . . seeks out the points where the great battles are fought . . . delights in the struggle between natural forces . . . love or hate, rebellious or social instincts'. His view of how *The Father* should be played fluctuated. He advised one Swedish company[5]: 'Not tragedy, not comedy, but something in between. Do not take the tempo too quickly . . . until it accelerates by itself towards the last act'. In 1908, at his Intimate Theatre in Stockholm, he advocated a very different approach: 'Grand, broad gestures . . . let loose the passions'; but the 1911 film of *The Father*[6] shows a generally quiet, subdued style of playing by the Intimate Theatre company. His mature view was: 'It is impossible to set up valid rules for theatrical art, but it ought to be contemporary in order that it may move contemporary people'.[7]

In fact, his Preface to *Miss Julie* sets out a justification for the kind of play he had written: highly concentrated in form, 'contemporary' in its analytical, sociological approach, yet also reviving features of the classical theatre in the single, uncomplicated plot, the compressed stage action which matches the passage of time in the auditorium, the lengthy monologues (like operatic arias), the chorus, dance and mime as elements of the drama. In what Strindberg says of his innovations in dialogue and setting, the naturalistic aim seems coupled with a rather different tendency. Thus he claims to have rejected the artifice of witty exchange in order to catch the actual movement of minds in everyday communication; but then admits to something like musical patterning in the verbal repetition and development of themes. His new concern for 'irregularity' in dialogue style seems matched with the visual 'asymmetry' he mentions (the realistic room shown only in part: the back wall running off at an angle, with the table set obliquely to it), a device intended to create unfamiliar perspectives and so lead the imagination of the audience to the unknown beyond what is seen.

What is unseen, but within the extended area the staging suggests, acquires an imminent presence in *Miss Julie*: the sexual act supposed to occur while the curtain is up and the scene continues; the suicide towards which Julie exits; above all, the return of the Count, Julie's father, signalled by the ringing bell, the speaking tube, and the symbolic power with which Jean's terror suddenly endows the boots that have stood in the kitchen from the start of the play. Stagecraft and theme correspond. The Preface refers to the 'slave mentality'; it shows in Jean's grovelling, not before a man (the father whose story Julie tells seems a poor stick) but before an impression in his own mind.

Strindberg claimed to be introducing a new technique of characterisation appropriate to an age of transition and to the modern understanding of how the chaos of social forces is manifest in the fluid, undefined nature of individual personality, 'characterless character'. An obvious parallel occurred later in D. H. Lawrence's rejection of 'the old stable ego of the character' for a new concept expressed in terms very familiar to Strindberg: of coal and diamond as allotropic states of the common element, carbon (letter to Edward Garnett, 5 July 1914). Strindberg's Julie, like so many of Lawrence's women, is a neurotic, whose unresolved conflicts are the product of social contradictions. Her ultimate fate is strikingly reproduced by Lawrence in an extended but basically similar fantasy of the Western, civilised woman who goes in a willing trance to sacrificial death ('The Woman Who Rode Away'). Like Hardy's Sue Bridehead, Julie takes the bold step forward towards sexual autonomy, and then regresses into self-immolation.

Strindberg was intensely interested in Neitzsche's ideas at this time, and followed Nietzsche in locating the slave mentality in women as well as servants. Unlike her own cook (the third character in the play), Julie does not know her place. Her sexual status and her social rank contradict each other and produce instability – from which the dramatic action takes its rhythm. The action takes place on Midsummer's Eve, through the long, Scandinavian summer twilight until dawn (Alf Sjoberg's award-winning 1951 film was able to exploit this). The Count is away and Julie is alone except for the servants who are celebrating the turn of the year with a harmless, if disrespectful, orgy. Julie wishes to descend and join in. Her flirtation with the valet Jean, who has pretensions above his station, is at least as much an exciting exercise of power for her as a response to her sexual instincts, roused by drink and the aphrodisiac perfume of lilacs. The peasants dancing on stage frame their coupling as the centre of a general fertility rite with clear subversive implications. The excitement ebbs, and the play goes into reverse. (Post-coital *tristesse* is a recurrent stage in the basic pattern of later Strindberg plays.) Even the fictional edifice collapses, as we can no longer tell what was and is fact from fantasy, lies from truth, – until the fertility rite is answered with a death rite.

Mesmerism, of great interest to contemporary neurologists, including Freud in his early career, provides Strindberg with a scientific metaphor for the ending of his play which also gives it a strikingly ritualistic effect: Julie sleepwalks to her death, moved, as it seems, by a will not her own. But the matter is more complex: she has had to direct Jean to impersonate the Master and order her to cut her throat, as if he were ordering a servant to sweep a floor (Jean '*takes the razor and places it in her hand*: Here's the broom . . .'). The initiative has come from Julie's class superiority; but she no longer believes in her individual power of self-determination and must go through this charade – Strindberg's vehicle to show how the internalisation of social patterns governs these beings – to deceive herself.

This is an entirely secular play, which presents psychological forces as the only genuine unseen powers. The Count is a mythical figure in the sceptic's sense, not God, but Godot already. *Miss Julie* marks a different stage from *The Father* in the dialectic of change: a temporary ebbing of the tide of social revolution, feminist or democratic. The retreat shown here actually reinforces the grip of a moribund patriarchy, a crumbling aristocracy. In the name of honour (defined in *The Father* as a male fiction, an empty nothing), Julie sacrifices herself to restore the old repressive order, but the Count's line is at an end.

Strindberg does not expound a thesis in *Miss Julie*, as Ibsen might have done, but his radicalism is contained in the play's intellectual structure, which gives it a peculiar hardness. This is the cage for a woman's role written out of his own androgynous feelings and uncertainties of class: as the son of a servant and her master, once a bankrupt. If he gave some of himself to the Captain, so he did to Julie, too.

Creditors does not have the tragic power of either *The Father* or *Miss Julie.* It is set, like the earlier *Comrades*, among artists, though the cast is now pared down virtually to three. In tone it is closely related to the subsequent group of plays (including *Debit and Credit* and *Playing with Fire*) to which Strindberg attached the label 'cynical'. The description is apt if we see in cynicism a refusal of emotion, as well as a barbed mockery of all idealistic expectations or interpretations. Gustav, who has carefully freed himself from all relationships of mutual or one-sided dependence and, finally, declares his preference for aloneness, with no wife or fiancée and no home, is the cynic of the play. He has adopted Schopenhauer's notorious definition of woman as his own:

> A half-developed man, a child stunted in mid-growth, a youth with udders on his chest, a case of chronic anaemia who has regular haemorrages thirteen times a year.
>
> (trans. M. Meyer I. 187)

What prompts the recitation is the figure which Adolf is sculpting: the nude, still faceless figure of a woman which stands on stage, sometimes veiled, sometimes revealed, as the play's central point of reference. Its value could not be better summed up than in the title of Buñuel's film, 'that obscure object of desire'.

Creditors is more mathematically conceived than *The Father* or *Miss Julie.* Like *Miss Julie*, it has a symmetrical elegance of design, but its analysis of human relationships concentrates more simply on a few psychic mechanisms. It is mostly a brittle comedy of the possessiveness of love and the absurdity of the marriage relationship. The objective view this implies is identified with Gustav as the author's surrogate within the play: the one who devises the plot, explains its development, and finally points the moral. He is even allowed to point to the element of chance in the work of art[8] (here taking the form of two ladies with no part in the plot who arrive on stage – a Pirandellian device to keep the audience aware of theatrical artifice). It is he who has persuaded Adolf (a painter) to turn to sculpture, arguing the value of supplying 'the third dimension' to achieve truthfulness. The term has a particular application in the action Gustav is devising: three characters disposed in a chain of pairs, three duologues with no intervals between, but each commenting on the third, invisible character.

This is a triangle drama in more than one sense. Setting out his plan to Adolf, in the first duologue, Gustav uses the theatrical metaphor to suggest another element, reinforcing the design: 'I shall take up my post over there in my room . . . while you act in here. Then, when the performance is over, we will change parts.' If the roles are interchangeable, perhaps they should be regarded as two aspects of man, or two male attitudes to woman and marriage. Indeed just before the end, the woman Tekla speaks of Gustav as Adolf's *doppelgänger* or *alter ego*. Adolf is emotionally involved, crippled in the dependency love has imposed on him; Gustav is disillusioned and therefore free, at an advantage with the woman who, we gather, was once his wife and with the man who discovers that this was his predecessor.

For Gustav, who claims to be simply the scientist-philosopher, 'at work dissecting a human soul and laying out the bits and pieces here on the table', is not disinterested but still involved, through his desire for revenge on the two who together 'betrayed' him. Like some of Strindberg's later characters (especially Hummel in *Ghost Sonata*), he has secretly assigned God's role to himself. The others are to be punished, and *are* punished when Adolf dies in Tekla's arms. Establishing the tone of Gustav's curtain line to the audience, 'It's the truth. She loves him too. Poor woman!' may well be the chief difficulty set by the play. We can see it, also, as the point towards which the whole production needs to be oriented. Strindberg wanted the audience to sympathise with all three characters. In so far as Gustav has borrowed the conventional role of *raisonneur* from the well-made play, the final line has authorial weight: the woman is to be pitied. But it comes from the same mouth which lied to mislead Tekla over what he knows has happened (Adolf's seizure) in the adjoining room:

> There's a table lying on its side and a broken water carafe. Nothing else. Perhaps someone has locked a dog in there. (trans. M. Meyer, I, 215)

It is possible to interpret *Creditors*, in the light of its moral ('innocent, but responsible') as a study of residual guilt, in which Gustav stands for the shadowy third who has always haunted the marriage of Adolf to Tekla, the one dispossessed, hurt and ridiculed as the price of the happiness they coveted. This is the sense in which Strindberg applies the metaphor of the creditor in subsequent plays. Uniting the functions of avenger and raisonneur in the single character, Gustav, links an act of primitive punishment with the deliberately staged clinical demonstration of a moral lesson. This points forward to Strindberg's more visionary work, which presents the spiritual punishments whereby souls are chastened through events of dubious reality resembling a play staged by an unknown author-director. Present-day Strindberg criticism is far from unanimous in emphasising the difference between the so-called pre-

Inferno and post-Inferno plays rather than the continuity from the earlier to the later.

Very short plays, known as *quart d'heures* became a feature of the Théâtre Libre repertoire. The best-known of Strindberg's exercises in this form, *The Stronger* (1889), reflects in its title the social Darwinist extension of the idea of the survival of the fittest to the human context. The application is quite playful, as the material is the stuff of fashionable boulevard theatre, an encounter between two women in a café, posing the question of which has the advantage in a triangular relationship, the wife, or the other woman? The play is also an experiment in performance art: a two-hander in which one part is wholly silent, and yet both actresses are required to be on stage and fully engaged with each other throughout. It is believed that Strindberg wrote both roles for his wife Siri: the speaking part for productions in Swedish or Finnish, the silent role for productions in other languages which she could not speak well. The result forces both actresses to play a subtext, as for one of them there is nothing else to play. Thus the limitations of the piece actually open up major and minor choices of interpretation, and different performances have led their audiences to opposite answers to the 'problem' posed. Strindberg here exploits the tendency to rivalry among actors (his plot has a theatrical context), whereby playing closely together involves playing for the advantage. Both in rehearsal and performance each actress has the opportunity to impose her interpretation of each moment in the script on the other: leading so strongly that the other must follow, or openly challenge and defy. Stage silence always has a certain weight. *The Stronger* is an invitation to the players to explore and exploit its enigmatic, disturbing, even threatening potentialities.

This is the most obvious instance of Strindberg taking

Zola's theory that the naturalistic writer should function not just as an observer but as an experimental scientist and applying it to the practice of his art as well as to the subject studied. In *The Father* he set out to find the breaking-point of a man, and created a stage symbol of this by forcing an actor to meet the challenge of some of the most sustained, complex and passionate speeches in the play while trussed and supine, while the others stand round and look down upon him. The spirit of 'what might happen, if we tried this?' informs the various technical experiments in *Miss Julie*, and the Preface emphasises the dramatist's wish to leave some freedom for improvisation in the long moments when characters are on stage without scripted dialogue to speak. His general artistic instinct favoured liveliness by allowing some space for the unpredictable. In 1894, he published an essay on the random in visual art, on which André Breton, leader of the Surrealists, commented many years later: 'Strindberg saw it all before us'.[9] It might have been said of his plays.

3
Out of Inferno

The next, and greatest, phase of Strindberg's playwriting career followed the period of mental breakdown which ended in 1897. Since 1892 he had been unable to write. Now the dam burst and, in under four years, 1898–1902, there poured out: *To Damascus* (Parts I and II, 1898; Part III, 1901), *Advent, Crimes and Crimes, Easter, The Dance of Death* I and II, *The Crown Bride*, *Swanwhite*, *A Dream Play*, and a whole cycle of seven history plays. None of these was a *quart d'heure* piece, or even a standard one-act play, but all were major in length, substance and quality.

The title, *To Damascus*, referring to the conversion of Saint Paul, signified a profound mental and emotional revolution. Essentially religious preoccupations take over, and the old naturalistic scepticism has a hard struggle to survive. Yet the interest Strindberg had taken in new tendencies in the visual arts and his understanding of how artistic perception and expression respond to new scientific concepts of the universe contribute as much to the new kind of play he now created. At first, he wrote *To Damascus* in two parts. These became the source of all the main features of dramatic expressionism which swept Germany on the eve of the First World War, dominated well into the 1920s and has remained an important element of modernism. What made the play so seminal was the combination of entirely modern ideas of multiple personality with a dramatic form derived from medieval theatre, breaking sharply away from the well-made play and the classical, Aristotelian tradition behind it, and – most vital – pervaded with a philosophic seriousness which no more precludes many varieties of humour than it does in Goethe's *Faust*. In a period of great intellectual and emotional upheaval, *To Damascus* appeared as a revelation of the lost and questing soul of humanity in an utterly perplexing universe, both equally unstable quantities.

Although the convention of act divisions is retained in the texts of Parts I and II, in genuine dramatic terms it has been replaced by quite different rhythms of development. Just as Strindberg preferred free verse forms to what he saw as the constrictions of metre and rhyme on a poet's thought and feeling, so he wanted the form of his play to follow the dictates of his imagination rather than confine and subdue it. However confused and chaotic the world may seem in the view he gives of it, the drama is controlled and shapely: unfolding, scene after scene, according to laws which are for the most part other than those of cause and effect.

From the experience of dreaming Strindberg had learnt how to dislocate our normal, waking sense of the passage of time: to make it seem to stand still, or even run backwards, showing events following each other in unpredictable sequence, or bringing back incidents for a rather different re-play. Ibsen's *Peer Gynt* and Strindberg's own fairy plays, *Lucky Peter's Travels* (1882) and *The Keys of Heaven* (1891), had been episodic and used many changes of set to mark the stages of a quest or pilgrimage. They had also moved to and fro between free fantasy and what might pass for realism in a folk-tale context. *To Damascus* was a much more significant departure. It was a major work which accepted the validity of dream as an essential part of human experience, and accepted the view of the world and the sense of human relationships emerging from dream states, or hallucinatory states, as fully admissible evidence in any search for truth: giving a reality at the interface of subjective and objective perception. The kind of relationship which links most of the characters in *To Damascus* had been anticipated outside drama, in the *alter ego* identities which preoccupied R. L. Stevenson in *Dr Jekyll and Mr Hyde*, in the relationship between Lord Henry and the hero of Oscar Wilde's *The Picture of Dorian Gray* and in Conrad's use of doubles, or mirroring characters, most subtly deployed in the relating of Marlow to Kurtz in *Heart of Darkness*.

However, introducing such doubles, or shadows, into drama had the technical effect of challenging, if not altogether abolishing, the convention of the realistic character pretending to be a living man or woman, whose family and social origins actors, critics and public could discuss, and whose personality could be psychoanalysed in search of motive. In fact, Strindberg was re-introducing the older concept of dramatic character as mask (allowing for the possible changing, or even interchanging, of masks by actors). Alongside this, he revived the medieval symbolic use of settings and, indeed, sometimes reverted to the medieval device of using simultaneous settings.

The protagonist of *To Damascus* is no blank allegorical generality (as the Man of some of Strindberg's Expressionist disciples tended to be); nor is he like the folk-tale heroes of the fairy plays, a Lucky or Unlucky

Peter. He has a history; certain memories haunt him; he is touchy, moody, yet capable of laconic self-mockery. His ghostly doubles have their own distinct voices, and this distinctness helps supply the play with its lively and energising conflicts. However, we are not meant to guess and piece together a fabric of realistic narrative. The exposition of the well-made-play has no place here (we have recently become accustomed to its absence from more modern plays and films). If there are lines which seem like unanchored remnants of such exposition, they are best treated as tokens of the substance and intricacy of a life, and followed here as they contribute to new, non-narrative patterns.

Critics have hesitated over whether to regard the Lady and the Doctor (a prominent figure in Part II) as characters in a different convention from the Beggar, the Confessor, or the Tempter, existing on a different plane of reality, closer to that of the protagonist. It could be said that the Lady and the Doctor (who at one point appears alongside the Unknown, identically dressed) seem to have the same kind of reality as other people have in our minds when they are physically absent, or the reality they have in our dreams (when the dead also have a kind of life). Something close to the ambiguousness of these figures occurs in Ibsen's later plays. Examples are the mysterious sailor to whom Ellida feels she has pledged herself, in *The Lady from the Sea*, and Hilde, in *The Master Builder*, who seems at once an independent character, a liberated young woman, and Solness's muse, or an image of youth conjured up by the strong attraction he feels to it, alongside fear. Perhaps the text of *To Damascus* tells us all we need to know: 'these are all illusions, and yet not just illusions'. Looking at the matter more technically, it can be said that the use of such characters restored to drama an advantage lost when modern naturalism had to exclude the ghosts available to Shakespeare as to Æschylus. The Grandmother, in *The Father*, whose stage existence is limited to a single call for attention, but who becomes an off-stage focus for ideas of the malignant will of the female sex, can be seen as a first step towards the invention of this kind of symbolic character; the unseen Count, in *Miss Julie*, would count as the next.

Along with the other innovations, Strindberg broke decisively with neo-classical ways of keeping tragedy and comedy as separate categories, to one or other of which a play might belong, but not to both. His protagonist, in *To Damascus* declares: 'Humour and earnestness are the same thing to me', which could be the epigraph for the trilogy and for the new, modern category of black comedy it introduced not only into drama (Franz Kafka was among Strindberg's literary disciples).

Eventually, *To Damascus* became a play in three parts, Strindberg's version of the *Divina Commedia.* Parts I and II corresponded to Dante's *Inferno* and *Purgatorio* and Part III to the *Paradiso.* (He strengthened the parallels as he went on writing.) However, Part I stands on its own as a complete, integrated and perfectly shaped morality play, yet it is also structured like a contrapuntal musical composition (as Strindberg himself asserted). Scene follows scene, linked by the repetition of ideas, themes, motifs, not by any superficial pattern of cause and effect (though we may ultimately find a hidden logic in the sequence). At mid-point in the play comes the major reversal, or conversion, after which the drama returns, scene by scene, through the settings of the first half in reverse order, until it finishes where it began: at the street corner near the Post Office, the café and the church, a mundane setting for the beginning and end of a spritual journey. After the rounded completeness of Part I, the second part comes as a surprise, as though Strindberg was uneasy to let a single statement, a single view, stand on its own, final and unchallenged. In fact, the repetitive and cyclic features of Part I are extended to a larger design. Part II is like another version, a different treatment, of the material of Part I, and its deliberately unresolved ending calls for a continuation. Part III was no continuation of the same plot, or direct development of the structure of Part II. Instead, the trilogy induces a sense of eternal recurrence: the struggle of life always resumes, after peaceful interludes, though it is not quite the same struggle each time, nor does it always take place on the same plane.

At the end of Part III, the central figure enters upon a ritual of dying into another life: 'You will lie in a coffin and pretend to die', says the Tempter, 'The old Adam will be exorcized with three shovelfuls of earth. . . . Then you will rise from the dead, having renounced your old name . . .'. This is a more explicit and unmistakable way of asserting the endlessness of life than through the ambiguousness of the stroke which leaves the Captain as dead at the close of *The Father*. In the hands of later playwrights, the cyclic form rarely contains the element of hope present in *To Damascus*, but *Long Day's Journey into Night*, *Who's Afraid of Virginia Woolf*, *Huit Clos*, *Waiting for Godot* and *Endgame* have not combined the idea of recurrence with that of a pilgrim's progress.

The translators into English of *To Damascus* have chosen to call the central character 'The Stranger'. This obscures the distinction between this character and the main figure in *The Burned House*, also called 'The Stranger'. In the later play this description corresponds to the Swedish *Främlingen*, whereas the protagonist of *To Damascus* is *Den Okände*, more precisely 'The Unknown' (used by some critics in discussing the play). This is no mere quibble, as the three parts of *To Damascus* also comprise the quest of a soul, or consciousness, which is the ultimate development of Strindberg's notion of the 'characterless character'. By lending the figure snatches of his own history, Strindberg has avoided the blank generality of an Everyman. Yet it is not the identifiable biographical details that make this a play of subjective experience, and to identify the Unknown with Strindberg is a gross error which actually obscures the form and meaning of the play. (He once thought of using Merlin as his central figure, a figure which had fascinated the leading contemporary symbolist, Villiers de l'Isle Adam.) Watching or reading the play, we ourselves embark on a quest, identifying with the Unknown to discover who the Unknown is. The other major characters serve as mirrors which present him (and us) with varying, partial, often contradictory images of the self.

In his manuscript, Strindberg represented the constellation of Orion as an image of integrated personality, and identified the satellite characters of the Beggar, the Dominican and the Confessor, in Part II, with the three stars of Orion's belt. (The Doctor and the Unknown appear identically dressed and share a particular relationship with the madman, Caesar.) With this evidence of the author's conscious intention, Evert Sprinchorn has interpreted Part II in Jungian terms and, while not essential to its understanding, his analysis of the play makes acceptable sense, a telling analogy to the original.[1] Sprinchorn identifies the Lady and the other female characters with aspects of the *anima*.

Part III expressly invokes Dante's Beatrice, and allusions to Goethe and to Doctor Faustus are hardly necessary to confirm that Strindberg was consciously representing the eternal feminine generally in the Lady and, in specific aspects, through the Mother and lesser female roles. At the beginning of Part I, the Unknown gives the Lady a name, Eve, and an age, as though he (a writer) was inventing her as a character; yet she is also addressed as Ingeborg. In Part III, he speaks of 'My bright hope, my dark longing, and my last prayer. To be reconciled with mankind through a woman –.' Clearly the status of the Lady, as a character, is ambiguous. Her reality is not solely objective or subjective, and she cannot be identified with any of Strindberg's three wives, although memories of his life with both Siri and Frida contribute to her particularity.

In Part I, the Unknown and the Lady set out on a journey, sometimes together, sometimes apart. Incidents and loose strands of narrative, and some of the figures encountered, correspond to experiences of Strindberg's second marriage which he built into a continuous narrative in *Inferno* (though the play as a whole is even closer to the autobiographical novella, *Jacob Wrestles*). Where the Unknown goes is determined by chance or fate rather than by design, though for an audience the sense of unpredictability yields, in the second half, to a realisation that he is retracing his steps through the same scenes in reverse order. Parts II and III do not have this predetermined structure of reversal. Though elements are still identifiable with material in the autobiographical novels, the action becomes more obviously and essentially mythic. Strindberg does not portray Frida or Siri, Dr. Eliasson, or Baron von Wrangel, but a series of protean and composite figures occasionally reminiscent of actual persons, who serve as guides or portents in a tangled spiritual destiny. The adventures of Faust, the journeys of Dante and Everyman are dominant models for the action of *To Damascus* Parts II and III.

The whole of *To Damascus* is concerned with spiritual blindness and illumination. Each of the three Parts has its own dominant and separate theme. In Part I, as later in *Crimes and Crimes*, Strindberg is concerned with the discrepancy between the human sense of justice and divine justice. The nature of his Inferno comes as close to Feodor Dostoievsky's thinking, in *Crime and Punishment*, as to Swedenborg's doctrine. By Act IV, the Unknown has begun to understand: 'There are moments when I believe that my sins and crimes are themselves my ordained punishments' (scene iii), and, in scene iv, he voices his longing 'for a torture to restore my sense of feeling equal with society so that I don't have to go on feeling in debt'. The theme of the changeling is worked through to the end when the Unknown is returned to himself. Part II moves on to another version of spiritual blindness, here the particular error of perception that translates a subjective sense of injury into a conviction of the malignancy of others, or cynicism which cannot distinguish good from evil. Part III is primarily concerned with love: the 'reconciliation with the world through a woman'.

At a crisis in Part I, the Unknown echoes the words spoken by Christ to Saul in his miraculous encounter on the road to Damascus: 'Saul, Saul, why persecutest thou me?' He is mocked for this spiritual self-aggrandisement (the quality represented in the play by Caesar) by the Beggar. It is in Part II that the Unknown is most conscious of his blindness (as Saul was physically blind for three days after seeing the divine radiance) and, as Strindberg commonly conflates myth with myth, thinks of himself as Œdipus. ('I wish I was your old blind father whom you could lead to the market-place to sing,' he says to the Lady.) Both the Doctor and the Unknown have drawn the lightning towards them, the latter in his Faustian role of scientific experimenter with electricity, and the Beggar links the notion with the course of repentance, the persecuting Saul converted into Paul preaching a new faith:

> You must preach against yourself from the rooftops; you must rend your web, thread by thread . . . But a man who has played with lightning is no coward. Oh, sometimes . . . you will be afraid – even of the stars, but mostly of the mill of sin, that grinds and grinds the past, the past, the past . . .
>
> (trans. M. Meyer, II, 167)

(Both the web and the mill are Swedenborgian symbols, the latter appearing again in the folk-tale context of *The Crown Bride* and in *Charles XII*.)

The composition of the dialogue of Part II (and Part III) is marked by the occasional long, developed speech among more realistic exchanges. That Strindberg had in mind the model of musical composition, with occasional sustained solo passages, seems to be confirmed by the very evident recapitulatory character of the last speeches of Part II, the entire purgatorial theme summed up in the Confessor's reading:

> The whole world shined with a clear light . . . over these only was spread a heavy night, an image of the darkness which would afterwards receive them. But yet were they unto themselves more grievous than the darkness.
>
> (trans. M. Meyer, II, 174–5)

Part III culminates in the entrance of a literally blind man among the characters, Father Uriel, whose name is explained ironically as meaning 'God my light', and who serves as the pretext for a long exposition of modern thought. This scene and the next, in which Father Melchior takes the Unknown round a portrait gallery which is a record of the development of Western civilisation from Boccaccio to Bismarck, are among the least stageably dramatic passages Strindberg ever wrote. (They are recognisably Dantesque and may be compared with the even more extended historical and philosophical expositions in G. B. Shaw's *Back to Methuselah*.) However, Father Melchior's conclusion is valuable for the clarity with which it acknowledges the principles, dialectical opposition and eternal recurrence, on which *To Damascus* (with some of Strindberg's other mature works) is constructed, and identifies their philosophical significance:

> The spirit of the age is promulgated by forces which are self-developing – *apparently* in circles. Hegel, the philosopher of the New Age . . . best solved the contradictions of life, history and the spirit with his magic formula: thesis, assent; antithesis, dissent; synthesis, marry the two . . . Say Both – And . . . or rather . . . Humanity and Resignation . . .
>
> (trans. M. Meyer, II, 258)

This may indeed stand as a summing up of Strindberg's own ultimate position throughout the post-Inferno years to the time of his death: with no millenial hopes for life on earth, he did not become indifferent to social questions, and his radicalism proved as strong in his last years as it had ever been.

Part II is dramatically the most powerful section of the trilogy. The dialectical balance of creation and destruction takes the form of interwoven plot-lines concerning, on the one hand, the Lady's pregnancy and the eventual birth of the child and, on the other, the Unknown's scientific experimentation, particularly the making of gold. The theme of human arrogance is denoted by the character of Caesar, who reflects this aspect of the Unknown, and is antithetically balanced by the Beggar. Caesar may well have a source in the similar character appearing in the Asylum scenes of *Peer Gynt*, which may also have provided a model for the climactic banquet scene. So, indeed, may Shakespeare's *Timon of Athens*, to which Strindberg's version of this ancient satirical motif (used subtly in *Macbeth*, too) comes closer. (He listed *Timon* among Shakespeare's most powerful plays.[2]) As in *The Father*, Strindberg places the male notion of honour in antithesis to the female power to bear children, and the Banquet is the public acknowledgment of fame, doing honour to the modern scientist who has achieved what experimenters have sought from the early days of alchemy. Yet fame and honour prove unstable fantasies, the splendours disappear, the dishes are whisked away, the guests slip out and the Unknown is left sitting among whores. Anticipating the potential of film, Strindberg asks for a scenic kaleidoscope – '*a landscape, a palace and a room*', before a prison cell settles into focus where, to the visiting Beggar, the Unknown declares, 'I think I was in hell. Or that I dreamed it all'. Part II of *To Damascus* is Purgatory, but Swedenborg's statement, 'Everything comes round again', corresponding to Hegel's idea of cyclic recurrence, implies that hell still returns at intervals.

Another repeated motif of *To Damascus* is based on Christ's last words from the cross, *Consummatum est* ('It is finished'), balanced both ironically and dialectically (as having equal validity) against the cyclic movement of the work. The kaleidoscopic effect is repeated at the end of the prison scene, thus emphasising the shift of perspective. The Unknown's words are answered by the Beggar: 'Wake up, then. Now you must face reality'. To the Unknown's question, 'Who am I fighting against?' he gives a reply that disarms what has been a common criticism of Strindberg's over-subjectivity: 'Adversity, like other men . . . Your own credulity, then?' (Meyer, II, p. 150).

The making of gold and the megalomania of the scientist are interpreted in terms of absolute destructiveness:

> I hold the fate of the world in my crucible, and within a week . . . all will be equally poor, and the children of men will creep lost around the earth like ants whose hill has been kicked to pieces.
>
> (trans. M. Meyer, I, p. 135)

Strindberg's personification of the mind in pursuit of power delivers one of the most striking expressions of our modern nightmare:

> Do you think I made gold to enrich myself? No, to destroy the order of the world . . . I am the destroyer, the annihilator, the world-burner, and when everything lies in ashes I shall wander starving among the ruins and rejoice at the thought: it is I who have done this, I who have written the last page of the world's history, which is now finished.
>
> (trans. M. Meyer, I, 136)

With the birth of the child, the Unknown becomes convinced of his own damnation, and Act IV of Part II is a dramatisation of the death-in-life which is cynicism. The end is quiet (*diminuendo*, in fact) and strikes a note of dark humour which anticipates Beckett, but contains an un-Beckettian hint of a purification undergone, a lesson usefully learnt:

UNKNOWN: There's a smell of corpses about.
DOCTOR: Perhaps it's us. (Meyer, II, 163)

Though Part III concentrates on the Confessor's guidance of the Unknown towards his grave, the counterpointing of death with new life returns: a child is carried to baptism as the Unknown, like Everyman at his end, steps into his coffin.

The patterning of the dialogue and all his directions for scenic effect, in *To Damascus*, testify to Strindberg's wish to invest drama with the flow and free emotional expressiveness of music. His intention was perceived by a major composer, Arnold Schoenberg, who carried it on through a number of musical compositions: the subjective monodrama *Erwartung* (1909), the *Totentanz der Prinzipen* (*Dance of Death of the Principles*, pre-1914), *Jakobsleiter* (first planned in direct response to Strindberg's autobiographical novella, *Jacob Wrestles*, though not executed for many years) and – closest to *To Damascus* in dramatic organisation – the opera, *Die glückliche Hand* (1908–13).

4
In a Higher Court

As the nineteenth century gave way to the twentieth, Strindberg was drawn, for a time, to the doctrines of the Catholic Church. He held back from full commitment to the Catholic communion, and the temptation to orthodoxy faded. Although he did not join the church, he thought at this time in deeply Christian terms and saw experience in the light of Christian faith and values. He had begun his Preface to *Miss Julie* with reference to the theatre as a 'Biblia pauperum' (including the modern theatre with the medieval, to which the term is more traditionally applied) as an art which reveals the truths of faith to the eyes of the unlettered. Following *To Damascus* Parts I and II, he wrote a number of plays, to which the 'Biblia pauperum' comparison applies with a new seriousness. In them he brings theatre and church, drama and Christianity together in various ways.

The titles, *Advent* and *Easter*, imply ritual plays for annual performance at particular seasons of the Christian year. Yet neither of these plays (and Strindberg also wrote a *Midsummer*) is an orthodox religious drama, viewing the world from the perspective of the church. *(There Are) Crimes and Crimes*,[1] which belongs to the same group, is most emphatically based on the secular world, through an action which takes place in Paris and features of style and structure which link it with fashionable boulevard comedies, well-made plays of strong erotic interest. The domestic setting of *Easter* recalls the typical small town scene of Ibsen's social drama and the characters have their ordinary, mundane concerns. The realistic fabric is unbroken, but each of the three acts is introduced by a passage from Haydn's *Seven Words from the Cross* which casts a mood of religious experience, associated with the period from Maundy Thursday to Easter Eve (the days when Christ lay in the tomb), over the life of the household.

The Symbolist project for assimilating the other arts to the structural and emotional qualities of music, aiming at a pure (and spiritual) aesthetic experience, influenced Strindberg's work very generally, but appeared in more marked and concentrated ways in his 'post-Inferno' plays. *Crimes and Crimes*, he stated, was structurally based on Beethoven's Sonata no. 17, and Evert Sprinchorn has analysed the play's thematic development to show its correspondence with the finale of the sonata, commenting: 'When bars 96–107 are heard as specified in the script, it is as if, for a few moments, the pattern broke through the tracing'.[2] The correspondence with a visual effect to be seen in a number of Strindberg's paintings is at least as striking: a juxtaposition of dark and light areas in an almost abstract composition. The sombreness of the first scene of *Crimes and Crimes* is in sharp contrast to the lurid glitter of the scenes of heightened consciousness played out between the playwright, Maurice, and the *femme fatale*, Henriette.

Between the opening of the play and the ending is an even greater dissonance.

None of Strindberg's plays begins on a more melancholy note, among the tombs in the cemetery of Montparnasse, while dusk is gathering. Dark cypresses form a background to the monuments. Another feature of the scene is a ruined windmill, overgrown with ivy (one of Strindberg's many versions of the mills of God). Human figures in the picture are dressed in black: a woman in mourning, praying beside a new grave covered with flowers, and the still figure of an Abbé reading a breviary. Strindberg had previously written an essay called 'In the Cemetery', and it is likely that he aimed at a similar evocation of mood in choosing the setting of the first scene of this play. The woman Jeanne paces back and forth, detached from the background by her movement, while her child plays with withered flowers gathered from a heap of rubbish. The flowers, we gather later, carry disease, and all the symbols of death anticipate the death of the child. The dialogue starts with the entrance of a verger to check the little girl, 'this is no playground'. The moment recurs in variant form later, when the guilty lovers are turned out of the Luxembourg Gardens by a keeper; and, at that point, the allusion to Adam and Eve driven out of the Garden of Eden is unmistakable. The echo emphasises the first scene's view of the world after the Fall as a place of death and corruption in which even children are soon infected.

It is a most unlikely beginning for a play that is to end as a comedy, in general laughter. Indeed the final lines expose the stage – unlike the cemetery – as a playground, as they point the artifice which ties up the divergent themes and gives the 'happy ending'. The term 'solution' is appropriate to a puzzle and also to a type of dramatic structure:

MAURICE: . . . my decision is made. Tonight I will meet you at the church to have a reckoning with myself about all this – but tomorrow I shall go to the theatre.
MME. CATHERINE: A good solution, Monsieur Maurice.
ADOLPHE: Yes, that's the solution. Phew!
(*Crimes and Crimes*, trans. Elizabeth Sprigge, *Five Plays*, p. 120)

The Abbé caps this with 'Yes, that is it', though 'tit for tat' would be a better rendering, echoing the verbal device of Strindberg's eventual title, *Brott och Brott.*

The narrative plots of this play and of *Easter* are alike in their half-resemblance to the conventional thriller of crime and detection. This was not the aspect of Edgar Allen Poe's 'The Gold Bug' which had especially roused Strindberg's enthusiasm and prompted the writing of *Pariah*, but the thriller-form of such stories as that and 'The Murders in the Rue Morgue' gave him models he now found useful. They are never wholly convincing as crime stories; on the contrary, Strindberg has cultivated a sense of unreality about the action in both plays.

Only in a nightmare would such a fuss be made about the disappearance of a bowl of daffodils from a florist's shop as brings an atmosphere of dread into *Easter*. The association of the daffodils with Eleanora, who first appears holding them, turns her into a modern version of the daffodil girl of myth, Persephone, for the spring festival to which the play refers is not exclusively Christian. It is equally hard to credit that, outside dreams, the police would be in pursuit of Maurice for the murder of his child, on such vague suspicions and absurd 'evidence' as are offered in *Crimes and Crimes.* The apparent action of each of these plays turns out, from the logical point of view, to be illusory, the equivalent of a play mounted for the benefit of the main characters and in which they are themselves centrally involved – as the author, indeed, came to feel about his own life. The implication that what has apparently happened has been a mysterious kind of hoax, and that Maurice's friends at the Crémerie, especially the proprietor, Mme. Cathérine, have been in on the secret, emerges quite strongly in the last scene of *Crimes and Crimes*, though the identity of the (divine?) joker, the hidden hand (perhaps simply that of the dramatist), remains uncertain. The huge silhouettes that fall on the drawn blinds, in *Easter*, are obviously part of a shadow-show for the benefit of human children who cannot bear too much reality, and the swish of his galoshes, announcing the avenging power at the door, identifies him as a fairy-tale ogre. It is not too surprising that he turns out to be a benefactor.

Strindberg personifies goodness, in *Easter*, in Eleanora, the girl from the asylum who lives in the spirit amid mundane reality (a portrait of his sister). His treatment of this character is a triumph of dramatic tact. Whether her slightly odd directness and her wisdom so distinct from common sense are symptoms of insanity is a question left open, when Elis and his fiancée Christina, watch her and Elis's schoolboy brother together:

> CHRISTINA: Do you think she's recovered now?
> ELIS: Yes. If it weren't for this exaggerated sensitivity of hers. She's sitting there now reading the story of Christ's agony, and sometimes she cries.
> CHRISTINA: Well, I remember we used to do that in school on Wednesdays during Lent –.
>
> (trans. M. Meyer II 295)

The character is left even more delicately poised by a suggestion that schoolboy Benjamin may be a little in love with her:

CHRISTINA: Ssh! Don't touch the butterfly's wings or it will fly away.
ELIS: They're looking at each other and only pretending to read. I don't hear them turning any pages.

Though Strindberg acknowledged a model favoured among symbolists – Balzac's androgynous Séraphita – Eleanora cannot, without outrage to the play, be pushed wholly into the category of symbol or the alternative of realistic insanity. Strindberg achieves an effect of visiting intimations of spiritual truth, not least because the impression of sunshine that Eleanora carries with her is shot through with sadness, a settled awareness of the sorrows of the world.

Strindberg anchors this pervasive sadness within the structure of the play through a plot-motif – of shady financial dealings – of the kind Ibsen favoured (e.g., in *The Wild Duck* and *John Gabriel Borkman*). Heyst, the father of the family, is serving a long prison sentence for embezzlement; the mock ogre is his principal creditor. Heyst, as Dis to Eleanora's Persephone, half-claims her and cannot himself be rescued as, within the enchanted ground of the play, the others escape the disasters they have feared. The parallel in *Crimes and Crimes* lies in the loss that is not repaired when Maurice, having been through hell in a paradigm, returns as a chastened man to his ordinary life to find his theatrical success secure, his friends rejoicing with him, but his child and his girl not restored. The child is dead, and no-one mentions or grieves for her in the final scene. The silence (given Strindberg's feeling for children) may be a measure of the spiritual unreality of common life, an indication of how it skates on the surface. Something jarring about the ending, the easy dismissal of Jeanne's grief and glib excusing of Maurice in relation to the vivid, uneffaced memory of the play's opening scene, is calculated to send the audience away still troubled. (The effect is such an irony as Shakespeare's *All's Well that Ends Well* achieves.) One of the sources of *Crimes and Crimes* was Kierkegaard's parable, ' "Guilty?" – "Not Guilty" ', in which the restoration of the young man to his former state ('Everything comes back') is similarly incomplete. Audiences do not need to be aware of this source to absorb the impact of the view Strindberg shares with Kierkegaard which could be summed up in Gustav's words from *Creditors*: 'Not guilty, but responsible'; in this case, excusable by the moral standards appropriate to men and women, while the whole of mankind is guilty in relation to God and within the spiritual universe. The death of the child, the event which is no illusion, corresponds to Maurice's sin of thought.

After *Miss Julie*, *Crimes and Crimes* is the most erotically charged of Strindberg's plays. It may be that his strong sense of guilt about sex, persuasively discussed by Gunnar Brandell, actually helped him present the excitement, glamour and dangerous intensity of the brief infatuation of Maurice and Henriette in a context where sexual temptation had to be linked with evil. During their mad, irresponsible night, Henriette ceases to be a woman like other women: she is possessed by a demon and aware of being raised above the chances and vulnerabilities of mortal life. Maurice hails her as 'Astarte!' baleful and enchanting deity of a pagan world. She has come to him as the seductive, female embodiment of worldly success, of fame as an author, which promises to raise him as a superman above the crowd.

The Faustian temptation of evil is given full theatrical heightening in *Crimes and Crimes*, and the most splendid of the play's settings, a restaurant full of mirrors made more unreal by its emptiness, matches the inflated emotion of Maurice with its own luxury. Strindberg's original title for this play was *Rus* (*Intoxication*, the German title being *Rausch*), a guide to the interpretation of the style as well as the content of the central scenes; for the lovers drink a metaphysical wine, having put human pity aside for the aggrandisement of their egoism. Certainly Paris was the setting of Strindberg's first theatrical triumph, but Paris is also a *mythic* city with precise literary and theatrical connotations.

Strindberg published the text of *Crimes and Crimes* together with that of *Advent*, under the common title borrowed for this chapter, *In a Higher Court*. *Advent* has been Strindberg's most under-estimated play, though it has inspired masterpieces including Kafka's *The Trial*. As theatre it bears little relation to the plays he wrote under the influence of the Naturalists and it is equally remote from classical models. It has a large cast and would be impossible to perform on a small, bare stage, for it depends as much on stage images as on dialogue. Edwin Björkman preferred to give his translation the title *Christmas*. The advantage of this is that it links the play with pantomimes and related entertainments. In his own day, it must have been evident that Strindberg was writing in the vein of Hans Christian Andersen's productions in Copenhagen, full of stage magic.[3] The other tradition of Romantic theatre to which *Advent* belongs is that of *Faust* and the attempts to stage Dante's *Divina Commedia*. Strindberg here presents the world directly as a spiritual place, with unbroken continuity between life and death, without the subjectivity, or egocentricity of *To Damascus*. The play's prevailing tone is wry and adult, and the emotions its images evoke are adult too. Altogether, the play marks Strindberg's reintroduction of imaginative richness to the stage.

Strindberg here presents the spiritual world directly, with unbroken continuity between life and death. The multiple symbolic set he describes for the first scene includes a newly-built mausoleum which gave the play its original title. The central characters, a retired judge and his wife, look on it as their next home. It is a deeply Christian play, though not theologically orthodox. It runs closely parallel to the *Book of Job*, it its general questioning of the possibility of human righteousness, in its theme of God's chastening of souls through afflictions, and in the ring of particular lines. It is a morality play in the mediaeval sense: starting with an examination of the soul when death is imminent, and proceeding through a vision of what is in store for it, opening the eyes of characters and audience to spiritual reality. It is not surprising to find his friend Gustav Uddgren commenting that Strindberg had been reading mediaeval drama at this time.[4]

To call the Judge and his wife, the Old Lady, hypocrites is to apply a gross name to a subtle fault. The Judge opens the play with an exemplary speech of gratitude for blessings received: 'Life's eve has at last brought the sunshine which its morning promised us. Early rains and late rains have blessed meadow and field',[5] sum it up in images of providential goodness. But these characters do not know that, like all men, they are sinners.

Strindberg had read *Job* with the aid of Swedenborg, accepting particularly the idea that sin itself is its own punishment. The Judge's peculiar sin is that he has been a just judge, according to the corrupt secular notion of justice as a matter of crime and punishment, as distinct from sin, expiation and mercy. ('Shall mortal man be more just than God?' is the challenge issued to Job.) So it is appropriate that he should suffer the illusion of such justice (as Job declares, 'Thou scarest me with dreams, and terrifiest me through visions'). He finds himself in such a world as Job describes, 'A land of darkness, as darkness itself; and of the shadow of death, without any order, and where the light is as darkness'. Here he encounters ghostly figures, some of whom bear an uncanny resemblance to himself (e.g. '*The Magistrate, dressed and made-up like the Judge . . . carries a rope around his neck*'), until this theme reaches its climax in a Court Room where the process of justice is carried through without visible agency: '*The bell rings. The gavel raps*' and ultimately the axe moves; 'Justice must take its course', declares the Judge, as though it was a force of nature outside human control. He meets a blind man who is also his own image:

> GHOST: I am not. – I have been . . . that unrighteous judge who is now come here to receive his sentence . . . Pray for me, you whose conscience is clear.
>
> (trans. E. Björkman)

The last sentence echoes ironically indeed.

Advent has a double action: although events on the

spiritual plane predominate, a thread of secular plot concerning the old people's relationship with their daughter Amelia, their son-in-law and their grandchildren, is consistently interwoven with them. What happens on one plane happens also on another, in a different guise. The formal division of the piece into five Acts corresponds to the strong dramatic sweep of the whole, but this general progress embraces a series of episodic dreams and a phantasmagoria of images. Dumb shows and processions betray Strindberg's acquaintance with Jacobean drama (for instance, in the way emblematic figures pass over the stage in Act I – the Auctioneer, the Chimney Sweep, the Lady in White, following Death with his scythe and hour glass, and the beheaded sailor – and return later in the play). Variations of tone are frequent.

In the first Act, the Judge and his wife encounter a series of guides, and their experiences are partly in this world, partly in the world of the spirit. Their own relationship shifts from harmony to dissonance. The second Act is set in the house of their life ('This whole dreadful house is nothing but secrets', says the daughter), a more cluttered anticipation of the house of *Ghost Sonata*, in which the harp and the clock are already prominent. At the end of a grotesque dinner, the Other One appears on cue and points the way forward – to 'an honest declaration of bankruptcy', through experience of evil and self- and mutual torture. Act III alternates episodes involving the children with others involving the old couple: the Judge and his wife are sentenced to separation, as they separated their daughter from her husband; and the figure of the Playmate, the Christ-child, appears in contrast to the Other One, but they do not encounter each other, and the heavenly world in which the children can play brings no joy to the old sinners.

Act IV is devoted for the greater part to the Old Lady, who attends a grotesque ball in Hell, where she dances in her finery with a hunchbacked Prince (played in the 1921 Old Vic production by Ernest Milton), – until her wig is torn off, revealing her baldness. This proves to be a dream within a dream, returning the Old Lady to the signpost in the woods where the Act began; but it is not the end of her ordeal, as she is sent on her way to 'walk in darkness . . . until you drop'. The last section of this Act is set in the Court Room where the Judge is condemned by 'process of law' and the Ghost announces the next episode, 'the big auction' (recalling the auction in *Peer Gynt*).

Although Act V returns to the house of Act II, the illusory nature of events is indicated as in the Court Room scene: illusory because it happens in the material world, where the old people's possessions are sold up after their death, but seen through spiritual insight; for the auction 'has already taken place . . . it was held elsewhere'. So the souls of those who are dead go through the process Swedenborg called 'vastation', a stripping and emptying of everything they were; and the process culminates in the Judge's being taken out to be stoned 'according to the Mosaic law'. The scene changes back to the edge of Hell, where the ball was held in Act II, though now it is called the 'waiting room' and is dominated by a pair of scales. The old couple are together again, sitting at a table, and there are signs that their spiritual blindness is lifting. The Judge is now conscious of events in the material world as a dream – he has dreamed his own burial; and he begins to realise that they are in Hell. It is Christmas Eve, and a time for special treats: 'an extra ration of rod all round' and the distribution of stereoscopes ('have a look in the peep-show . . . There is your whole life story and all your victims'), medicinal gifts.

The central pair are permitted a vision of Amelia and her family re-united, and for themselves it is the beginning of hope, which comes first to the Old Lady. She takes her husband's hand before the tableau of the Magi as the Christmas crib appears to them and all the shadows around them, including the Other One himself.

For the Other One, whose chief disguises in *Advent* are the garb of a down-at-heel schoolmaster and the robe of a Franciscan friar, clings – like the water sprite in *The Crown Bride* – to a remote hope of redemption. Evil is not absolute, any more than human goodness is unblemished. This is a play with music, and music, sometimes heard and sometimes silent, is among its chief symbols. The Old Lady plays the harp, and the Other One thanks her: 'It lulls the pain and awakens memories of better things, even in a lost soul'. The musicians play for the ball in Hell, but nothing is audible: 'It's splendid, but they might play a little more *forte*' is the Old Lady's comment. Strindberg's versions of Hell are frequently and intentionally comic.

There is certainly grimness in the play, too, and tenderness. Amelia and her husband are never much more than lay figures in the old people's dream. (If the husband's situation is identified, along bio-critical lines, with Strindberg's own – and the old people have been identified with Frida Uhl's grandparents –, it has to be admitted that the biographical material is kept at a distance and not developed at all.) In keeping with the author's general view that human beings are not naturally wicked, but are made so by their experience of life, he presents the children as undivided beings, who can live simultaneously in spiritual and material worlds, accepting the presence of the Christ-child in the sunshine as children accept the playmate they so often invent for themselves. Yet they are guilty of their own small sins and are punished through the agency of the Old Lady with her birch rods: punished and warned as Alexander is, in Ingmar Bergman's film, *Fanny and Alexander*, in a fantasy action that is a kind of game. Certainly *Advent* and Strindberg's following plays provided the groundwork for Bergman's linkage of theatre and religion by a technique of controlled yet multitudinous fantasy seen in his early morality film, *The Seventh Seal*, equally with *Fanny and Alexander* which takes its epigraph from Strindberg.

5
Dramatist as Director

Visual Imagination

No dramatist has ever given more consideration to the visual dimension of his plays than Strindberg. His introduction of Arnold Böcklin's painting, *The Isle of the Dead*, at the end of the late play *The Ghost Sonata*, to impose a mood of unearthly tranquillity and ultimate solitude, was the climax of a long practice of using the scene, the stage picture, expressively. He was well equipped to do so, having been a practising painter. His pictures are well represented in Scandinavian public collections, but have only been seen outside Scandinavia in an exhibition of 'Sources of the Twentieth Century' at the Paris Musée National d'Art Moderne in 1960–61, and in a small travelling exhibition which visited the British Museum in 1962.

While in France, he was in direct contact with other painters who were breaking new ground in the recording of their personal visions. Grez, near Fontainebleau, where he settled with Siri in 1883, was an artists' colony, and they returned there in 1885. Here, he met the Norwegian, Edvard Munch, and Paul Gauguin. During the mid-1890s in Paris he associated with Gauguin regularly at the Crémerie in Montmartre which is featured, only lightly disguised, in *Crimes and Crimes*. The Czech artist, Alphonse Mucha, also frequented the place at the same period. Munch turned up there again and painted Strindberg as the gaunt central figure of his nightmarish picture, *In the Clinic*. He painted Strindberg's portrait in 1892. The well-known lithograph showing the head surmounted with a jagged margin and the figure of a woman, elongated like a spermatozoon under a microscope, completing the border, belongs to 1896.[1]

The account of Sellén's picture, in Chapter Six of *The Red Room*, closely matches the author's own work:

> The subject was simple and grand. A stretch of drift-sand on the coast of Holland with the sea in the background, in autumn mood, the sun gleaming through broken clouds. Part of the foreground was of drift-sand with newly washed-up, dripping seaweed, lit by the sun, then the sea, part of it in deep shadow, but with high white-crested waves, while in the background the sun was shining again on the horizon, opening up perspective to infinity. The only live thing was a flight of birds . . . the mood had dictated the colour, not the other way round.
>
> 'You should have put something in the foreground', Lundell instructed him. 'Put a cow in the foreground.'
>
> 'You're talking rot,' Sellén replied.
>
> (trans. Elizabeth Sprigge)[2]

Strindberg sometimes painted trees. One picture shows buildings: far away and minimal in scale, they focus a band of sunlight on the horizon, across a great stretch of water. It could well be a dream city. There are no cows and no human figures to disturb the solitude in any of his compositions. The sea in all its moods, or sea and sky together, were his favourite subject. He acknowledged J. M. W. Turner as his master, but his pictures also strikingly anticipate the abstract colourism of our own day. He used a much less chromatic palette than Emil Nolde in his sea studies and his canvases are further from the conventionally pictorial. The exclusion of human and animal figures enabled him to produce works that had rhythm in the irregular patterning of colour and texture (he liked to use a palette knife), yet seemed to be amorphous, with no external form but the conventional rectangle of canvas or board. Yet even this is challenged in the double composition that has a dark rectangle inset in a larger area of predominantly pastel colours. He offers the visual equivalent of the literary or dramatic 'slice of life', but of elemental life, an undifferentiated chaos.

Some of the pictures are calm, though they may be cut sharply across by a horizon line; in others the pigment is churned up and presents violent contrasts of light and dark, sea indistinguishable from sky. One late group of paintings recalls the Fingal's Cave scene in *A Dream Play*, or the principle of the *camera oscura*: the light is focused on a central oval, or mandorla roughly defined, as though the sea were viewed from within a dark grotto or through the opening in a dense framework of leafy boughs. There may be a hint of flower forms tumbled in the waves, as in Böcklin's *Isle of the Living* or certain pictures by Odilon Redon. Although the Stockholm archipelago, with its thousands of islands and skerries, gave Strindberg the model to paint from, as it gave him the rocky fortress setting for *The Dance of Death*, the title of one stormy seascape, *Night of the Jealousy*, strongly suggests that he was painting an inner world of emotion as well. 'The amusing thing is that I was the first to paint symbolic landscapes and now the whole pack of realists have turned with the wind', he wrote to his violinist friend, Leopold Littmansson, in 1894.[3]

Delius was genuinely impressed by the Swede's accounts of his scientific labours, but disconcerted when Strindberg brought out a photograph of Paul Verlaine on his death-bed and urged him to see the huge beast lying across the body (a tumbled pile of bed-clothes) and the crouching devil on the floor (a fallen pillow). *Inferno* testifies to Strindberg's awareness of how greatly his superstition conflicted with his empirical scientific background. Yet it was a creative imagination, freed from the filter of consensus interpretations of the visual world, that allowed him to read, like a fanciful child, a visionary landscape into the markings left on the zinc bath he had used for his alchemical experiments. The fantastically shaped, burnt coals he poked out of the fire, drew and then set out on his table, where they were mistaken for sculptured forms, have been identified by modern critics (who also draw parallels between Strindberg's painting, and of Kandinsky and Kupka) as the first examples of *objets trouvés* in modern art.[4] Scientists were using new technology to discover totally unfamiliar views of the material universe, and Strindberg had photographed the sky as seen through a telescope, crystals viewed under a microscope. With the eye of faith searching for omens, the hero of the autobiographical novel, *Inferno*, studies the germination of a walnut, in a period of anxiety about his wife and child, and interprets what he sees through the lens: 'two tiny hands, white as alabaster, raised and clasped as if in prayer' (Chapter 5, trans. Mary Sandbach).

August Strindberg

Strindberg's essay 'Des arts nouveaux' (published in the *Révue des Révues*, 15 November 1894) includes an account of how he painted: his intention scarcely half-formed, inviting liveliness from spontaneity – as in his writing – and expecting the viewer to participate in turn, progressing from the first impression of a chaos of colours to creative interpretation. Strindberg uses a favourite metaphor: spectator combines with artist in a procreative act.

He had always been interested in the machinery of visual illusion. In *Old Stockholm*, recollections published in 1880–82, Strindberg gives an account of Chinese shadow plays and shows an illustration of one.[5] In the newspaper *Svenska Dagbladet*, 21 January 1899, he referred enthusiastically to shadow plays he had recently seen at the Paris cabaret, the Chat Noir. The power of the magic lantern is the basis of the crucial episode in *Tschandala*: 'By means of this it was possible at will to evoke light pictures on walls, on smoke, or any other background of fairly solid consistency'. In 1889, Strindberg wrote of his idea for a fantasy play set during the French Revolution, using a large magic lantern. He was, perhaps, influenced by some account of Etienne Robertson's phantasmagorias which seemed to conjure up the ghosts of Voltaire, Marat and other heroes and victims of the Revolution for the entertainment of their citizen contemporaries. He was convinced that similarly projected pictures could solve the problem of creating the spiritual and dreamlike effects required for the staging of some of his later plays, and brushed aside the objection that fairground devices might cheapen the production. Insisting on his readiness to learn from all kinds of sources, he declared, 'I first learned at a circus what an unexpected effect one can get by painting the scenery on transparent fabric'.[6]

Like many of his contemporaries, he became interested

in the development of photography and experimented with it. In 1892, he even thought of becoming a professional photographer as a way out of his financial difficulties.[7] The family photographs and self-portraits he took at Gersau, when he was living there with Siri and the children in 1886, remain an intimate and charming record of one of the happier times in his life. Later, he experimented with double exposures and trick photography as well as making camera studies of cloud formation and other phenomena connected with his scientific experiments. He wrote several pieces on his photographic studies, and 'Le ciel et l'oeil' was published in the Paris journal *L'Initiation* in May 1896. As early as August 1886, he had mentioned in a letter the *revolver photographique*, capable of taking twelve pictures per second. Much later, in the second volume of his *Blue Books* he noted, 'how many shots must be taken in sequence by the cinema photographer to reproduce a single movement, and even so the image is blurred. There is a missing transition in every vibration'[8] – and compared the writer's technique of characterisation. This new consciousness of what is involved in motion that the film camera brought, invites comparison with the Italian Futurists' – especially Boccioni's – importation into painting of effects seen in multiple exposure and stroboscopic photography to give a new sense of speed within static, two-dimensional art.

Cinemas were sufficiently commonplace in the cities of Europe in the early years of the 20th century for Strindberg to refer to films as a more 'democratic' form of entertainment than the theatre and to tell the players at the Intimate Theatre of his critical thoughts on the theatre's retention of old forms without adapting them to the needs and expectations of the modern age. He was an occasional cinema-goer himself and was thus familiar with the anti-naturalistic possibilities of film-editing and projection, including the effects of slow motion or comic acceleration. The new kinds and contrasts of dramatic rhythm that enter into his post-Inferno plays, the kaleidoscopic succession of scenes after the turning point in *To Damascus* and *A Dream Play*, the more staccato development of *Ghost Sonata*, were surely as much a response to the challenge of new technology, and how it might be affecting the processes of human perception, as to any personal disorder of the senses.

It was only to be expected that, when Anna Hoffman-Uddgren was filming *Miss Julie*, in 1911, Strindberg should think of writing a piece especially for the cinema. Julius Regis ('Should Strindberg have written for the Cinema?', *Filmjournalen*, 1922) was reminded by the *World-Historical Trilogy* (the three late plays on Moses, Socrates and Christ) of D. W. Griffith's masterpiece, *Intolerance.* Indeed, if Strindberg did have some notion of film production in mind, that might explain the sketchy writing of those plays. But it is safer to assume that the silent film epics had some influence on certain of his major history plays, especially *The Saga of the Folkungs*, *Gustav Adolf*, *The Last of the Knights* and *The Regent.* This was not an instance of inadequately copying what film could do better, but of making the theatre a more exciting place through imaginatively expressive and ingenious developments in dramatic style. Any debt was fully repaid when the German Expressionist movement, acknowledging Strindberg's paternity, realised itself in one of the most creative periods of film art, and a more personal debt has been paid in the film career of Ingmar Bergman.[9]

A Theatre of his Own

Strindberg had hankered after a company and theatre of his own from at least 1876 and, just over 10 years later, he made overtures to August Lindberg, who had staged Ibsen's *Ghosts*, in the hope that together they could start a touring company. Strindberg promised new plays for the repertoire and a leading lady, his wife, Siri. In 1889, two years after Antoine's founding of the Théâtre Libre in Paris, he opened at the Dagmar Theatre, Copenhagen, with premières of *Creditors*, *The Stronger* and *Pariah*. The two shorter plays, specially written for the occasion, were well received, but *Creditors* shocked the audience into derision. The enterprise had already been fatally damaged by the banning of *Miss Julie* literally on the eve of its opening, for this was the play on which the dramatist had mainly staked his hopes and which should have started the season. It was a very brief season as a result: postponed for a week until 9 March, it did not survive into a second week, for Strindberg simply did not have the resources to carry on. The work on *Miss Julie* did not go entirely to waste. A private performance was arranged at the Students' Union of Copenhagen University on 14 March. The audience numbered 150. The playwright himself watched in off-stage concealment with the extreme nervous anxiety that was in future to keep him away from all public performances of his work. Siri played Julie, as she played Madame X in *The Stronger* and Tekla in *Creditors*. Apparently the hauteur she gave to Julie exceeded the passionate human feeling needed for the part. In 1892, Strindberg was again planning for an experimental theatre, now in the Stockholm area, and wrote for it *The Bond*, *Debit and Credit*, *The First Warning*, *Facing Death* and

Mother Love. Nothing came of this, except that the stock of plays available for performance was increasing.

The Strindberg theatre finally came into being through the agency of a young actor called August Falck, son of a housemanager of the same name at Dramaten who had played the lead in a production of *The Father* at Josephson's New Theatre in Stockholm. August Falck the younger, born in 1882, had toured as an actor in Sweden and Finland and had also been financial manager for a theatre at Helsingfors in 1902–4 before setting up his own company to tour Sweden. The outstanding item in their repertoire was *Miss Julie*, a considerable success in its first production to be seen in Sweden. After presenting the play to some acclaim at the People's Theatre (Folkets Hus) in Stockholm, in 1906, Falck made his approach to the dramatist. The story of what followed is told in his untranslated book, *Fem År med Strindberg* (*Five Years with Strindberg*). His edition of notes sent by Strindberg to individual actors at their Intimate Theatre was published with Introduction and commentaries under the short title of *Strindberg och teater* (*Strindberg and the Theatre*) in 1918.[10]

The premises eventually leased at Norra Bantorget 20 were more cramped than anything Strindberg had previously had in mind. Even so, the general ideal of what a theatre building should be was not sacrificed, though everything had to be on a miniature scale. Advance publicity in the form of interviews with the Stockholm press and the publication of sketches showing the attractively furnished and carpeted Smoking Room (with portrait of the author on the wall) and Ladies' Salon (containing the bust of Strindberg) as well as the auditorium, stressed the elegance and comfort of an environment where patrons could discuss the play at their ease. The auditorium contained stalls only: a total of 161 seats arranged in 15 rows, including 7 armchairs at one side, leaving an ample gangway the other side. The ceiling was draped with yellow silk, through which the lighting was softly dispersed. At the front of the auditorium, on either side of the curtained stage, hung copies of Arnold Böcklin's two symbolic pictures, 'The Island of the Living' and 'The Island of the Dead', the latter being Strindberg's favourite painting.[11] (Together they must have seemed emblems of a poetic theatre, more symbolist than naturalistic.) There was also a greenroom and a remodelled store as well as dressing rooms. After noting these conveniences, it comes as a shock to realise that the dimensions of the stage were approximately 20 feet wide by 13 feet deep (6 × 4 metres). The forestage was gently curved. There was nothing of the shabbiness or austerity usually associated with 'fringe' theatre in all this, but the restrictions on staging accepted for the sake of the rather luxurious surroundings were to turn the production of some of Strindberg's more demanding works into tests of ingenuity rather than challenges to imagination.

The basic lighting equipment consisted of footlights and a batten of improvised spotlights. (Strindberg's plea for cross-lighting, in the Preface to *Miss Julie*, could be satisfied.) They were able to position three sets of wings, but fire regulations ruled out any possibility of shifting one scene to reveal another already in place, and it was a complicated matter to bring items out of the store along the corridors and past dressing rooms to the stage.

In the summer of 1907, the dramatist made a number of proposals to Falck that would set their theatre apart from ordinary commercial theatre of the time. There would be no prompter and no orchestra (only music as part of the play). The evening's performance would be limited to about two hours (8.00 p.m.–10.00 p.m.), with brief intervals or none at all, and calling for actors to receive applause during the course of the play would be banned. Smoking would be forbidden, and there would be no Sunday matinées. Playscripts would be on sale in the theatre. There seems eventually to have been a small buffet, though Strindberg had earlier thought to exclude a bar.

The company gathered by Falck was young (he was only 25 himself) and generally inexperienced. Throughout the four years of the theatre's official existence, there was a permanent core of half-a-dozen actors, including Falck himself. Manda Björling, who was 31 years old in 1907, had been on stage for six years and had been a member of Falck's previous company. (They married in 1909.) She played the female leads in many of the plays although, true to the democratic ideals of this kind of theatre, younger actresses often took over the parts from her. The fact that Falck himself nearly always played Strindberg's heroic roles is probably an indication that they were beyond the capacity of the other men at this time. Most actors came for one or two seasons, making a company of 13 or 14 players, increased to 17 in 1909–10. Anna Flygare (who had a great success as Eleanora in *Easter*, and also played the Baroness in *The Bond*, Alice in *The Dance of Death*, Swanwhite and Jeanne in *Crimes and Crimes*) remained at the Intimate Theatre until January, 1910. Fanny Falkner, whom Strindberg wished to make his fourth wife, was first noticed by him at Intiman as a Page in *Sir Bengt's Wife*, in 1908, and went on to play Swanwhite, Judith in *The Dance of Death*, and Agnes in *Storm.* (Harriet Bosse, his third wife, never acted at Intiman; she was the Lady to August Palme's Unknown in *To Damascus* I at Dramaten in 1900 and played Indra's Daughter in *A Dream Play* at the Svenska

Theatre in 1907, while the Strindberg–Falck venture was in active preparation.)

Five plays were presented in the first season, late November to the end of December, 1907: *The Pelican*, *The Burned House* and *Storm* (all 'chamber plays' specially written for this theatre), *Miss Julie* and *The Stronger.* The theatre was open from January to December over the next three years, and a considerable part of Strindberg's *oeuvre* was presented, including plays of contrasting types from all periods of his writing career. Many of these were receiving their first production, in Sweden at least. Those best liked by audiences were carried over in production from one season to the next. In addition to *Miss Julie*, eight plays were mounted in 1908: *Ghost Sonata* (a chamber play); *The Bond* in a single programme with *Playing with Fire* (one of Strindberg's few comedies) or with *Pariah*; *Sir Bengt's Wife*; *Kristina*; *Easter*; *The Father*; and *Swanwhite. Crimes and Crimes*, the two parts of *Dance of Death* and *The Secret of the Guild* (another medieval play) were introduced into the repertory in 1909. Additions in 1910 were: *The Great Highway* (a pilgrimage play), the naturalistic *Comrades* (including the remarkable character of Abel, the androgynous 'new woman'), and the short pieces, *Facing Death*, *The Outlaw* (an early play, set in the Viking Age), *The First Warning* and *Creditors.* Part I of *To Damascus* was included in the final season, and so was the only play by another author, Maeterlinck's *L'Intruse.*

In all, 134 performances of *Miss Julie* were given at Strindberg's theatre, 152 of *Swanwhite* and 182 of *Easter. The Father*, *The Dance of Death* and *Kristina* were next in frequency of repetition. The company played guest seasons in Denmark and Norway, as well as in Göteborg; members of the company visited Uppsala to play there on Strindberg's sixtieth birthday, and *Swanwhite* was given an open air performance before a huge audience in Adlesnäs Park at midsummer in 1909 (evidence of the acceptance of Strindberg as Sweden's national playwright). Several other productions had been planned but not brought to the point of presentation: productions of the folk play, *The Crown Bride*, and of *Abu Casem's Slippers* (in preparation when the theatre closed down); while Strindberg had returned constantly to the problems of mounting *A Dream Play* in the cramped conditions of the Intima stage with many ingenious suggestions as to how they might be solved.

The dramatist's mind was occupied with theatrical practicalities to the last detail, drawing on personal observations, experience from his involvement in the staging of his plays at other, larger theatres, and ideas which came from a wide reading of books and articles on the history of staging and on contemporary theatrical experiments in other countries.[12] He was enthusiastic about German innovations in staging; he was familiar with Gordon Craig's and Appia's theories of stage design and was particularly responsive to ideas of how light and colour might be used in new ways in the theatre. From his study of staging methods used in the theatres of earlier periods, he came up with many ingenious suggestions for their adaptation to meet particular needs in their own productions. In the early days of the enterprise, Strindberg and Falck were engaged in almost daily long talks in the former's apartment; and these were supplemented by the multitude of notes the dramatist sent to his young colleague.

Gordon Craig had issued his challenge to the actor-dominated theatre in 1905, announcing the coming of a new theatrical art in which the imagination of the director would have full control. Faced by the prospect of playing Adolf in *The Father*, Falck proposed that Strindberg should himself take on the office of artistic director – Max Reinhardt was currently making this new concept more familiar through his work at the Deutsches Teater and Kammerspielhaus in Berlin. In his initial enthusiasm for theatrical intimacy, the Swedish dramatist identified the project he and Falck were developing with Reinhardt's experiment with a small theatre. Such small theatres could certainly be regarded as merely the latest in the line of semi-professional, avant-garde organisations set up in the 1880s and 1890s which had had to accept the necessity of performing in halls and basements not originally intended as theatres. However, Reinhardt was not so pressed; he already had his main auditorium, and the Kammerspielhaus was intended for an extension of his work in the direction of intimacy, at the other extreme from his attempts to revive the mass theatrical spectacles of the medieval or ancient world in Salzburg Cathedral or London's Olympia exhibition centre.

In fact, Intiman, though part of the Independent Theatre movement to outflank the orthodox nineteenth-century theatres and commercial managements and introduce new methods of staging and styles of performance for a truly modern, new drama, was not one of its earliest manifestations. Antoine had been at work in his own theatre since 1887; the Moscow Art Theatre had been founded by Stanislavsky and Nemirovitch-Danchenko in 1897; the Irish Players had opened the Abbey Theatre, Dublin (with a stage 21 feet wide at its maximum and 16 feet deep), in 1904; Granville Barker had shown London the value of creative play-direction at the Court Theatre, 1904–7.

Certainly a small-scale independent theatre operating regularly in Stockholm was a new thing for Sweden, and it was the realisation of ideas Strindberg had harboured for many years: a theatre which would bring players and audience closer together and would preserve the intensity of the dramatic experience. He and Falck subscribed to what were now the orthodoxies of the new movement: ample rehearsal time; a company without stars, in which actors would not monopolise particular roles, but would shift freely between small parts and leads, and were trained to play harmoniously together in the service of the dramatist's text; the avoidance of the old rhctorical and exaggerated acting-style and cultivation of a quieter style, seeming more natural, yet precisely controlled. The unique feature was the theatre devoted exclusively to interpreting the work of a single, modern author. (Of course, several theatres had become the regular medium between a particular author and his public, as with Chekhov, Maeterlinck or Bernard Shaw.)

Strindberg took his obligations as a director very seriously, though he came to regard the special appointment as unnecessary and relinquished it after a while, perhaps largely because he shrank from continued attendance at rehearsals. While *The Father* was in preparation, he was to be seen in the stalls, silently watching and listening, preferring to communicate with the actors individually and privately, sending them little notes of comment and advice, unfailingly courteous. He showed himself very sensitive to the actors' predicament, recognising their need for praise and encouragement to counterbalance negative criticism, and also acknowledging the difficulty they might sometimes have in grasping what the director wanted them to do: 'I suspect that the actor acts so unconsciously, so much like a sleepwalker, that he literally does not understand what the director says.' Ultimately, he was always ready to withdraw a demand and leave it to the player's sense of what was right, 'Give the actor as much freedom in his work as possible', he advised, 'otherwise he will remain a pupil all his life' (*Letters to the Intimate Theatre*, trans. W. Johnson).[13]

Indeed, he put his responsibility to the members of the company at least as high as the claims of his plays. Nothing else will explain the nature of his Open Letters to the actors, intended as lectures, but which he was too shy to deliver in person and therefore had circulated in written form. These are not directly concerned with the forthcoming production, but broaden out from hints on technique to contributions to the complete education of an actor: taking pains to explain the aims of the enterprise they were engaged in, its relation to the theatrical context and the reason for some of its practices; encouraging an understanding of, and respect for, their art and mutual consideration and cooperation among themselves; introducing them to some of the great classics of drama, and a range of his own (historical) plays beyond the works they were actually to perform, and analysing some of their qualities; discussing principles of stage design, the art of stage speech, how to prepare a role, even looking at theatrical economics in a survey of the current theatrical situation in Stockholm. These letters are very informally structured, unpretentious and even intimate in tone.

Strindberg warned the actors against over-complicated techniques and against 'reading too many books about the art of acting'. He put *concentration* first among the elements of that art and *imagination* second, having no doubt at all about the actor's creative contribution to the play, and going into details on how others should avoid breaking an actor's concentration in performance. On the other hand, he continually emphasised the importance of clear and beautiful speech. He insisted that the actor's personality should serve the role, not dominate it, and condemned the hardening of character-parts into caricatures: 'The character is, of course, the essence of a human being's *inner* life'. (LIT trans. W. Johnson) Yet, while agreeing that good acting involved '*being* the character portrayed intensively', he was careful to add: 'but not so intensively that he forgets the "punctuation".' Phrasing intonation and variety of rhythm were never to be neglected – he liked to use musical terms, *crescendo* and *diminuendo*, *accelerando* and *ritardando*. At first, a teacher of elocution was employed, but this was abandoned in order to move towards a more natural delivery, befitting the dimensions of the theatre even more than the types of play presented there. Still, Strindberg's advice to particular actors to keep their speech within the most pleasing part of their vocal register, or to speak the syllables *legato*, like pearls on a necklace, suggest an aesthetic concern rather remote from the 'method' naturalism of a later day.

With the authority of the author, he could make the occasional straightforward statement about a character's nature or feelings. Thus, in *Easter*, 'The old man should be gentle, benevolent and only *pretend* wickedness'; Eleonora 'has discovered her "destiny" and resigns herself to it. She sighs at moments but doesn't complain'. Yet there is no psychoanalysing of character, only reflection on the value of observation and allowing feeling to be the mainspring of the acting: 'If the actor's whole being is suffused with his character, the character is expressed in every muscle, every nerve, every tendon. The gesture follows the word quite naturally, all the muscles tingle.' He emphasised the importance of mental and emotional activity, the silent acting of listeners, as long as they remain on stage: 'I have seen the cook listen to Lady Julie's death fantasies about an imagined happy future in such a way that I have had to applaud the cook'.

During much of the existence of this Intimate Theatre, Strindberg and Falck seemed to maintain a successful balance of opinion and approach. Falck's sense of the difficulty with which *The Dance of Death*, Parts I and II, challenged the young company, resulted in the calling of eighty rehearsals, so that the work might be prepared with the utmost thoroughness. Strindberg intervened to prevent this becoming a regular practice, warning of the danger of losing spontaneity and naturalness through over-rehearsal.

Many of the notes Strindberg sent to Falck give the impression that the dramatist was straining towards new modes of presentation which would bring all his plays within the compass of their theatre's resources, while the records of production indicate how Falck matched the honest and unpretentious acting they arrived at with a practicable décor, tending more towards simplicity than ingenuity. He accepted many of Strindberg's suggestions, and the latter generally expressed approval – sometimes enthusiasm – for what Falck achieved. At first, in keeping with his opinion that 'a naturalistic play can be presented only naturalistically', the dramatist thought of the sets as rooms which they were setting up and furnishing on stage (some production photographs show a false ceiling with suspended lighting behind the flounced proscenium border) but rooms which could create a mood, as well as enhancing the artistic effect of the play. He praised the *art nouveau* style and colour of the room Falck, on his advice, provided for the first production, *The Pelican*: 'There was something else in that room; there was atmosphere, a white fragrance of sick room and nursery, with something green on a bureau as if placed there by an invisible hand.' A photograph of *The Father* in performance shows a similar, rather surprising, effect of light given by the pale walls, symbolically decorated with military weapons.

The problem of how to mount one of Strindberg's large-scale history plays at Intiman led to the most important shift in their approach. Inspired by the revolt against nineteenth-century scenic productions of Shakespeare, especially in Germany (Strindberg refers to the Shakespeare stage introduced by Karl von Perfall in Munich towards the end of the 1880s), they realised the advantages, beyond mere convenience, in giving some plays a purely conventional or abstract setting. Falck presented *Kristina* in drapes, thus demonstrating the possibility of doing without the precise detail Strindberg had imagined and embodied in the stage directions for his historical plays. Arguing that the realistic settings were not missed by the audience, Strindberg saw this as a way towards the dramatic effect he desired in other plays: too literal and material an approach to staging *Ghost Sonata* had missed the effect he was seeking, whereas the style of the play might be better suited by avoidance of such localisation – they must try again. Playing *Easter* in curtains would be a way of ridding an essentially spiritual action of 'all material trappings'. The change was not made in this instance, but later performances of *Swanwhite* substituted curtains on which lights played for the original set based on Knut Ström's charming design, which was probably difficult to realise effectively on so small a stage.

Strindberg's aim was now 'de-materialisation', far removed from the realism he had advocated in the Preface to *Miss Julie*, when he was reacting forecefully against the obvious falsity of a tired convention. The rejection of painted sets was not a move in the direction of austerity, as it was accompanied by a new emphasis on colour and special lighting effects: 'We have . . . discovered the red velvet drapes can take on all the nuances of colour, from azure blue, through molten metals to purple, simply by applying varied lights', he recorded. In his plans for putting on *A Dream Play* he broke away from the idea of localisation in any particular period in his advocacy of colourful costumes in a mixture of styles from all ages, 'Because here in the dream there is no reality', they would be justified in making beauty their goal.

What he had learnt of medieval staging, renaissance theatrical devices, seventeenth-century staging at the Hôtel de Bourgogne, as well as his reading about contemporary experiments in other countries, and previous discussion of methods employed in the staging of his plays at other Stockholm theatres, provided him with an inexhaustible abundance of practical ideas. He suggested the display of decorative emblems as a method of scene location (e.g., in *Kristina*), or a variety of ways in which scenic elements or symbols might be combined in a composite decor (or 'simultaneous' setting) to be used throughout the play; turning columns (suggested by the periaktoi of classical theatre); winding and unwinding backcloths; ways of giving depth (and metaphysical perspective) to the stage picture; properties which could be converted to various uses as successive scenes demanded (like the hatstand–candelabrum in *A Dream Play*); the projection of pictures on to a backcloth (as in the final moments of *Ghost Sonata*). He insisted that the showmanship of popular entertainments was as worthy a source of techniques to make the theatrical medium more fully expressive of the meanings in the play as the researches of scholars and visions of idealists in the arts.

Together with the delight he expressed in so much that Falck achieved, Strindberg undoubtedly suffered repeated disappointment at Falck's resistance to tackling an even greater range of his most ambitious plays. His exasperation was expressed when a planned presentation of *The Crown*

Bride, on a visit of the company to Dalarna, was cancelled by Falck on the grounds that it would have put excessive strain on the players at the end of a tiring season. Offered so many suggested lines on which a production of *A Dream Play*, Strindberg's dearest wish, might be tackled Falck dragged his feet, and eventually came up instead with a sensitive, effective version of Maeterlinck's quietly suspenseful, one-act play, *L'Intruse*, worth doing in itself, and well within the little theatre's capacity.

Although Strindberg had proposed, before the theatre was launched, that they should make it a theatre of classic plays, including works by Euripides and Racine, as well as outstanding modern plays (and he had come to admire Maeterlinck's work greatly) Falck's insertion of this particular play was among the factors that brought their joint enterprise to an end. Certainly they seemed to have established Intiman as a Strindberg theatre, and any deliberate policy of broadening its repertoire surely called for a specially designed season, in which a number of different authors would have been represented.

Strindberg's visions of what the theatre might become, prophetic of so many later twentieth-century developments, burst the confines of the collaboration. Behind him, certainly, lay the Wagnerian theatre giving so widespread an impetus to scenic experiment (though Strindberg disliked Wagner as a composer), but the possibilities he saw also reached out towards the Brechtian theatrical revolution.

Intiman closed its doors prematurely on 11 December 1910, yet it had made its mark. Enough had been done in over a thousand performances of twenty-five plays to establish the dramatist's stature. Reinhardt was aware of the aptness of Strindberg's work, not least his later plays, for his own adventures in stage direction, and he travelled to Stockholm to show the Swedes a new way ahead. Intiman had itself become a place of pilgrimage: for Bernard Shaw, whom Strindberg entertained to a private performance of *Miss Julie* and who did not realise how rare it was for the Swedish dramatist to attend a performance and the honour it implied; and for Gordon Craig himself (in Stockholm with Isadora Duncan) who had a rather different reception, a glimpse of the reluctant, beleaguered playwright through the aperture of a door.

Pär Lagerkvist, the Nobel Prize-winning author, in an article of 1918 on Strindberg's contribution to the art of the theatre, concluded that the playwright's vision was frustrated in the attempt to adapt his more ambitious plays to the small, conventional stage of Intiman; and he argued that the way ahead was through a return to the implications of the dramatic texts.[14] To modern directors and actors, the long and detailed descriptions of setting, costume and movement, especially in the history plays, may seem perverse and hampering to their own necessary creativity; though for a reader they are helpful reminders of how largely a play's meaning comes alive in a visual composition, and how other aspects, not least the rhythm of the playing, may modify the words spoken. Strindberg, writing these passages, was thinking like a director as well as a dramatist.

6
History Plays

At the height of his powers as a dramatist, Strindberg wrote a series of plays to form a cycle of Swedish history. The number of plays and the way they are interlinked show an extended scheme of some magnitude, and the varied, yet generally high quality of dramatic interest to be found in all parts of the cycle establishes Strindberg as the greatest historical dramatist of modern times, comparable only to 'my master Shakespeare'. The finished cycle starts from the late Middle Ages and finally brings Swedish history to the verge of the modern age.[1]

Even this is not the sum of his historical drama. The other works fall outside the national cycle and have their parallels among the early, less generally known plays of Ibsen. Like Ibsen's *The Feast at Sølhaug* and *The Vikings*, Strindberg's *Sir Bengt's Wife*[2] is transitional in its exploration of aspects of modern consciousness, and especially modern dilemmas of marriage and the social relations of the sexes, within the framework of period drama. Again, Strindberg, writing later, has perhaps moved further in his use of the life of a medieval convent, and its abolition by Reformation forces, as half-symbolic of the psychological as well as social changes of a later day. Strindberg's Margit prefigures Miss Julie as Ibsen's Hjördis points the way to Hedda Gabler.

Behind Strindberg's high valuation of spontaneity and 'naturalness' in writing, and the speed at which he wrote most of his work, was a counter-balancing capacity for study. In fact, when he came to write his plays, he could do so out of considerable resources of knowledge and thought about the art he practised. He had studied the craft of the well-made play, as he studied Chinese in his capacity as assistant librarian in the Royal Library. Now he turned to the systematic study of Shakespeare, seeing in his work the great alternative to the European classical tradition of drama which had latterly run into the sand in the French drama of society. Whereas a lesser artist would be tempted to reject one tradition in favour of the other, Strindberg continued to recognise that there was strength in both. As he insisted to the Company of his Intimate Theatre, they were 'two different approaches, the one as good as the other'.

The only Shakespeare plays known to Strindberg through performance were *Hamlet* (seen c. 1886) and later *Macbeth*, *Othello* and *A Midsummer Night's Dream.* He had first been introduced to Shakespearian texts through their use in class as a basis for study of the English language. The translations of Shakespeare's plays into Swedish by J. Hagberg, published from 1847 onwards, gave him a clearer and more immediate sense of what the plays were really like. He read Hagberg's introductory essays and notes with close attention. In some instances he went back to reading the original English texts of the plays, from the Temple editions. His own writings on the plays reveal a wide, if not always deep knowledge of Shakespeare scholarship and criticism and show special awareness of the traditional English appeal to 'nature' as opposed to 'art' in explaining the pre-eminence of a dramatist who so ignored classical precept and example. He was knowledgeable about the stage-history of the plays and the degrees of adaptation or butchery the text had undergone. He also had a strong practical interest in theatre history generally, which served his own work beyond the bounds of the history plays. He possessed and used well a general history of the theatre by H. A. Ring, published in Stockholm in 1898, and was informed about the contemporary movement favouring a return to the principles of Elizabethan staging for productions of Shakespeare.[3] Strindberg's discussions of *Hamlet* support his statement to the actors at the Intimate Theatre that he had read at least twenty commentaries on the play.

Not surprisingly, *Hamlet* first roused his enthusiasm and gave him a deeper personal interest in Shakespearian drama. He was perfectly aware that the play had become important to him because it showed him an image of his own emotional nature and psychological situation, his own attitude to maternal and paternal figures, his own ambivalence to woman as lover, his sense of alienation from society. Yet he did not leave it there: as a professional dramatist he became intensely interested in Shakespeare's artistry. His comments on Shakespeare's dramatic techniques show his awareness of the Elizabethan dramatists' inheritance from medieval theatre; on the other hand, the musical terminology he applies to Shakespearian plot-construction, for instance, is that of late nineteenth-century symbolism, as in the comment, 'There is a fugue in the action, where Laertes picks up and carries Hamlet's voice, but in the bass (Hamlet was a tenor)', and when he sums up the general composition of the play, 'It forms a symphony, polyphonically developed with independent motifs, which are beautifully woven together'.[4]

Shakespeare gave him a useful precedent for justifying his 'transcendence' of historical accuracy and preference of symbolic ('conventional, universal') time to archaism; for selecting and rearranging historical incident to suit his theme and give relevance to his own day; for realism in the presentation of character, settings and incidents of common life; and for the introduction of vigorous, often colloquial, language. When he first wrote *Master Olof* in prose, he was unable to get it accepted for performance because its idiomatic everyday dialogue offended conventional taste, as its verdict on Olof as a renegade offended pious nationalism. He revised and rewrote, compromising to the extent of leaving the modern thrust of his prose for a more 'elevated' verse dialogue. When he returned to writing historical drama twenty-five years later, he deliberately picked up the threads of his original method, but with the benefit now of a more extensive knowledge and better understanding of how 'my master Shakespeare' worked. His appreciation of Shakespeare's realism, and of the prominence given to the common people in his plays, led naturally to Strindberg's use of popular sources for his own historical drama: folk ballads and traditional tales as well as the standard academic authorities. He had built up his familiarity with such material, drawing particularly on A. A. Afzelius, *The Saga Annals of the Swedish People* (1881), while preparing his prose work, *The Swedish People*, which appeared in 1882.

A pattern of thematic echoes (sometimes involving parallels between Biblical and secular history) knits Strindberg's series of plays into a true cycle of many constituent parts. His focus on anniversaries, significant days in the calendar, aligns the facts of history with mythological time.

Strindberg's debt to Shakespeare was never that of the mere imitator and artistic traditionalist; the lessons he learnt from his 'master' had a particular appeal to a modern mind and lent themselves to the expression of modern ideas of history. Strindberg had read Buckle and, as a 'naturalist', absorbed his view of history as an evolutionary process, while Buckle's emphasis on masses rather than individuals as the makers of history appealed to Strindberg's radical and democratic tendencies, fusing in his imagination with the prominence Shakespearian history gives to low-life characters. However, it is questionable whether Strindberg ever saw history as a purely secular matter.

His choice of Olaus Petri, the prime maker of the Reformation in Sweden, as protagonist of his first major attempt in the genre, confronted him with the theme of conflict between secular and religious power, both in the public arena and within the consciousness of the individual. Shakespeare's interest in God's design working its way through the dynastic quarrels of the English monarchy was a constant guide to the Swedish dramatist, as the Hegelian idea of cyclic recurrence became assimilated in his mind to his post-'Inferno' conviction of some higher power, governing events and overriding human will. This fatalism is most strikingly illustrated in *Erik XIV* when Counsellor Göran becomes spiritually aware of what is happening, stops striving to control events and turns into a passive spectator of destiny acting on and through people and circumstances. In the essay, 'Världhistoriens Mystik', Strindberg formulated the more complex conclusion he had reached after the failure of his attempts to discover any satisfactory explanation of the historical process on solely national lines. He refers to 'the discovery made long ago that historical development is controlled by certain laws resembling those that govern . . . nature', and adds, 'One . . . must recognise human will to a certain extent, and . . . necessity', then he looks beyond to 'the great synthesiser', 'the invisible law-maker'.

This general meaning informs all parts of the cycle to some degree, yet the individual plays have their separate themes and distinct structures. Strindberg matches these to the cultural character of the particular period that concerns him, though he follows no single procedure in making this match. *The Saga of the Folkungs* recalls the strongly visual and emblematic quality of medieval theatre in its pageantry and its concentration on grouped characters rather than isolated individuals. *Gustav III* is structured on a metaphor of theatrical performance and masquerade, taking its cue from the cultural interests of Sweden's eighteenth-century playwright-king and the society he led. High comedy is the style appropriate to the Enlightenment, and so Strindberg does not follow the King's reign to his death, though he introduces Gustav's ultimate assassin to shadow the happy ending in reconciliation and escape from danger. *Kristina* looks out of seventeenth-century extravagance towards the late nineteenth century in its treatment of the modern theme it shares with *Miss Julie*: of a woman made neurotic by the conflicting social forces that box her in, torn as she is through the opposed roles that meet in her, here the power, authority and responsibility of a hereditary monarch, undermined by a traditional feminine dependence, vanity and need for love. Strindberg was inspired to adapt Shakespeare's presentation of Cleopatra, her temperamental rages, swift transitions, vacillations alternating with arrogant absolutism, as majestic poses dissolve to reveal a shivering slip of a girl: not a 'lass unparallelled' in Strindberg's version. For Kristina is an actress by necessity, a 'characterless character' in the negative sense, null and lost behind her masks, while the brilliant variety of

Cleopatra is the self-realisation of the born player. Kristina (as a social portent) is the chief character in her play. In *Gustav Vasa* and, even more, *Charles XII*, Strindberg flouts traditional Swedish idealisation of the hero-king by keeping the titular character off-stage, or stressing his human fallibility, even deficiency, and focusing on the nature of the power each stands for, more than on the monarch himself. (Because the plays take their titles from Sweden's monarchs, it is sometimes wrongly assumed that Strindberg interpreted history in terms of great individuals.)

Strindberg's anti-militarism, which fuelled his hatred of Charles XII, interpreted the earlier warrior Gustav Adolf as a reconciler, an actor on the vast stage of European strife and intrigue – extending, indeed, beyond Europe into other continents and faiths – who pointed away from nationalism towards internationalism and from sectarian intolerance towards the fundamental unity of all religions. Strindberg was attracted to the idea of European federations, and *Gustav Adolf*, which he referred to as his *Nathan the Wise* (Lessing's masterpiece), was certainly addressed to his own day. (It is probably that *Gustav Adolf* and perhaps *Karl XII* too influenced Brecht's *Mother Courage*.)

Though it is an impossibly long play, the individual scenes and sections of *Gustav Adolf* are generally gripping and mostly as stageable as anything Strindberg wrote; and a fair number of the vast list of characters come vividly to life. The history plays, indeed, contain the majority of the strong male roles in Strindberg's drama. *Gustav Vasa*, for instance, presents a gallery of contrasted personalities, having each a forceful and stable ego, various manifestations of the firm and unifying government of which the Vasa king is figurehead. In this instance, as generally through the history plays, Strindberg's abhorrence of stereotypical characters moves in combination with the principle he found in Shakespeare, that he is 'always deeply engaged' and 'embodies himself in the person who is talking at the moment'. Thus the audience or reader is drawn into empathy even with Charles XII, and the experience of turning reluctantly from one character, until the next makes an equal claim on our emotional and intellectual interest, is a common effect of all the plays. Even when, as in *Erik XIV* and *Kristina*, he sets out to present a weak human being, the characterisation is compelling, and as much his own concept of the monarch in the case of Erik as of Charles. Given the historical clue of the possibly false accusation of madness brought against Erik the courtly poet and ruthless politician of popular imagination, Strindberg drew a psychologically complex figure, like Kristina endowed with the neurotic quality of a modern character, and again drawn in part from a Shakespearian model – this time, Hamlet. A passage in *Open Letters to the Intimate Theatre* (pp. 80–1) draws attention to the relationship of the two characters, and it is his interpretation of Hamlet as both feigning madness and actually toppling into that condition wich is the basis of his drawing of Erik. The structure of *Erik XIV* reflects a recognition that Hamlet acts both hero and fool in his own play: 'he talks as Yorick would have done' among the graveyard fools (in his 'retrospect on all of life as the great nonsense'), even fulfilling the fool's function in that he 'sings out what all the others think'.

The first (prose) version of *Master Olof* was prepared over five years, on the tide of a radical cultural movement, and rejected by Dramaten in 1872. The revised version of 1876 shows major changes of content, as well as a change to verse: Strindberg had reinterpreted history and changed his view of his central character. A year later, he added a striking Epilogue, including a pastiche of a medieval

Creation play which puts forward ideas that recur, many years later, in *Ghost Sonata.* A version of the prose *Olof* was presented at the New Theatre, Stockholm, in 1881; the verse play had its première in 1890 and was revived in 1920 in a famous production by Per Lindberg with designs by Knut Ström, when the Epilogue was performed for the first time. Both versions have remained in the repertoire.[5]

In the Red Room gives a semi-fictional account of the play's genesis and records other titles Strindberg considered giving to it: notably, *What Is Truth?* and *The Renegade.* He followed Shakespeare in combining elements of grotesque comedy with his heroic action, elements sometimes parodic of the main situation. Specific reminiscences of *Hamlet* and *The Tempest* are easily detected. The minor characters of the Sexton and his Wife stumble on the drunken sea captain Windrank, and Strindberg's use of an imagery of the sea and of drowning strengthens the resemblance of the episode to Stephano and Trinculo with Caliban. The first scene of Act V is set in the churchyard at St. Clara's convent and opens with Windrank and Nils, clearly like the Shakespearian gravediggers, counting the corpses of those dead of the plague. Olof, stepping on to a grave, confronts a procession of monks and nuns in a blending of the scene of Hamlet encountering the mourners at Ophelia's funeral with Richard III stopping the funeral procession of Henry VI. It is not the substance of the Shakespearian scenes, but the theatrical images they offer that Strindberg incorporates in his play, where they are as integral as Shakespeare's own adaptations of source material. They take their place in a succession of powerful images: the sudden appearance of the two Black Friars, like a filmic imposition on Olof's departing pupils (who represent his own childhood); the sudden opening of the iron door in the church wall to frame the figure of the Prostitute, in her black and red skirt, with a nun's veil over her head, and the ambiguous figure of Gert, the anabaptist stationer, beside her; Olof with Gert in the pillory outside the Great Church, while the bells ring, the organ plays, and his pupils process past to confirmation.

Gert is Strindberg's free invention, filling the silence of history: introduced as the father of Kristina, Olof's wife, he appears by turns a prophet, a licensed fool (he carries a certificate of health in anticipation of being taken off to the lunatic asylum), a satirical tempter, a symbolic figure of the revolutionary spirit. Through him and through Windrank, the dramatist multiplies perspectives on Olof and his achievement. In his uncompromising human character, Gert is taken off to be hanged at the end of the play, when Olof himself has been ransomed by the burghers, recants, and makes a political compact of loyalty to King Gustav Vasa. So tragedy appears to be averted, but to ironic effect: the boy Vilhelm, not realising that Olof has been released, salutes him as a martyr, and Gert's disembodied voice is heard, counterpointing the political justification the play has offered with the other possible verdict, 'Renegade!', as the curtain comes down. This double verdict, recognising the ambiguousness of history, is a striking anticipation of the variant endings of Brecht's *Galileo*. Another parallel between the two works is the imagery of gluttony, most vivid in the verse Olof and culminating in the appearance of Olof in the Epilogue, looking on at the inset play: a fat and complacent cleric, who now cares more for his creature comforts than for the transmission of his ideas ('his mouth has become empty as his stomach has swelled').

The biblia pauperum,[6] or pageant, aspect of *Master Olof*, and the Epilogue's device of the play-within-a-play giving a double perspective, return in *The Saga of the Folkungs*, the most operatic and spectacular of Strindberg's plays, yet filled out by Strindberg with a more subjective action recalling *To Damascus*. An artful pastiche, more like Marlowe's *Tamburlaine* than Shakespeare, *The Saga of the Folkungs* anticipates Bergman's film, *The Seventh Seal*, in its crowded canvas, the fantastic medley of images and the stamp of a creative personality whose private vision and emotional landscape give intensity to the work. The contrasts are daring, as in the shift from the masked ball and the theme of troubadour love back to the market place where a corpse hangs from the gallows and King Magnus parades his repentance, carrying a crucifix, flanked by Grey friars and followed by dancing flagellants, who in turn collide with a party of roistering buffoons playing their own music on kettle drums and pipes. Among the apocalyptic symbolism, nothing is more eerie than the mime of the Plague Girl, dressed in black, with a white cap, her face and hands painted scarlet, who chalks her mark on the doors and sweeps the place with her broom. A distinctly tart portrayal of Sweden's St. Bridget as a self-opinionated businesswoman is one of the features which give the play its modern perspective. The theme she is allowed to state, near the end, reveals a connection between this play and *Crimes and Crimes*: 'Sometimes, you see, we get off with merely a shock, and God often punishes us through our imaginations'. Magnus, the good man who has been a weakling, does, in fact, survive his own Christ-imitating pilgrimage: the tragedy has turned out to be a divine comedy, after all – and a spiritual warning.

None of Strindberg's works surpasses *Gustav Vasa* in masterly assurance and control. The material confronting him covered a reign of nearly forty years (1523–60) filled with significant incident. He had dealt with one aspect of it, the Swedish Reformation in religion, in *Master Olof*. Centring his new play on the King entailed seeing the

Reformation from another point of view, as one strand in a continuous programme to build a united and independent country. He chose to concentrate on a period mid-way in Gustav's reign and on a decisive struggle between the King and a force of commoners backed by foreign powers, including the Emperor and princes of the German states. The rebellion took place in Småland, on the Danish border, which had been the ground of conflict some half-dozen years before, and Strindberg manages to load the incidents and relationships of the play with the implications of past events, weaving the mesh of destiny in which all are held. The leader of the rebellion does not appear in the play; his is a name to be whispered, an identity to be hinted at, representing a potent, yet mysterious threat. More surprisingly, Strindberg goes half-way to keeping his hero out of the play too.

The first act is superbly theatrical. The location is Dalarna, region of strong independent traditions, to which the Småland rebellion is spreading. The first setting is in the house of Måns Nilsson, a friend to Gustav in the past and a leading member of those Dalesmen who have come to doubt whether his interests are compatible with theirs. So much is quickly conveyed in the opening moments of the scene, while Måns talks with his wife, who is setting out the silver in the King's honour. A bell is dully and dolefully tolling, a poor substitute for the copper bells taken by Gustav and handed over to the free city of Lübeck which financed his earlier wars. The children enter, dressed in black and white, and strew the floor with spruce twigs, as though for a funeral. Måns rehearses them in what they are to say to the King – words to remind him of old friendships that he has betrayed. The walls of the set are decorated with paintings which bring incidents from earlier years of Gustav's reign graphically into the room. (The last picture –

of the skier Engelbrekt, who bore the name of 'the great national leader of a hundred years ago' – anticipates the climax of the last act when 'the finger of God' unexpectedly introduces this Engelbrekt again.) At the head of the long table, centre stage, is the high chair ready for the King. Måns rehearses his daughter Barbro in the ballad she is to recite to Gustav when he sits there – a reminder of past loyalties of the Dalesmen to their king. Despite the period setting and the tension, there is a simple domestic intimacy in the scene.

Strindberg builds up the suspense: other leading Dalesmen gather at the house with news, or rumours, of the King's approach, and their unease, doubts and fears are given terse, subdued expression. The sound of muffled drums grows louder, followed by imperious knocking on the door. It is Master Olof, now the King's Secretary, and Herman Israel, representative of Lübeck, who enter, announcing Gustav's arrival in the vicinity, delivering his greetings and the message that he will summon those he wishes to see one by one to the Guild Hall.

The pretext that he does not speak Swedish allows Strindberg to keep Herman Israel silent and he gives weight to his silence by placing him in the high seat. It is left to Olof to talk with Måns and the others and to open the door when a messenger arrives, calling first for Ingel Hansson, then later for Nils of Söderby, the third time for Stig Larsson. Much of the dialogue is oblique; it is evidently Olof who has the upper hand and keeps the others in play, while they wait, increasingly apprehensive, until the drums are heard again, the messenger comes in once more – and flings three bloodstained coats on the table. The scene set for the King has been occupied by his deputies until the action has happened off stage.

Strindberg brings about a shift of focus at this point in

Act I. We have been emphatically involved with Måns, responsible, shrewd, brave; now, when Olof and Israel are left alone, they speak sympathetically of the Dalesmen, the guarded manner, the political mask, is put aside; and, as we become drawn to *them*, a larger perspective of Måns and his friends emerges. In Act II, the interest shifts again to Prince Erik and Herman's son, Jacob Israel, then to Göran Persson, friend and counsellor, whose vulnerability is momentarily revealed. Thus, when King Gustav finally appears in Act III, he is less the undisputed protagonist, in whose drama all the other figures are subordinates and instruments, than an alternative focal point, no less and no more interesting as a human portrait than any other – except that, as the King, he carries a responsibility for them, and the meaning of their lives and actions is subsumed in his. For Strindberg gives a double view of Gustav, detaching the kingly role a little from the man, as if he were an actor a little grotesquely, almost comically playing a god, Odin or Thor, yellow-haired and blue-cloaked, with his boar spear and war hammer. The caricature is pointed up by Strindberg's descriptive comment: '*the most striking* [painting on the wall] *depicts "God visiting Abraham in the grove of Mamre". The Abraham closely resembles the king*'. Yet Gustav's manner and personality are unpretentious, regal though he looks, and authoritative as he is able to sound. The husband, father, friend are realistically portrayed. Prince Erik's democratic sentiments – 'It seems to me . . . that people are equally good or bad everywhere' – are illustrated in the dramatist's handling. (Quotations from W. Johnson's translation of *Gustav Vasa*)

Strindberg, however, has more to say than this and, though *Gustav Vasa* shows a considerable grasp of the complex politics of a historical situation, the period setting and characters ultimately serve to objectify an impersonal theme, a spiritual drama which has close connections with *Advent* and *To Damascus*. Gustav, like the Judge in *Advent*, is a Job figure, subject to judgment 'in a higher court' and to a spiritual punishment and purgation. The executions of Act I, representing all the brutalities his achievements have cost, have to be expiated. In the course of Act IV '*the stage becomes darker*', and the action becomes symbolic: the King, seated on a bench in the square, is surrounded by beggars who do not recognise him (an incident that could have come from *To Damascus*) and then approached by Barbro and her mother, now Måns Nilsson's widow; they do not know who he is, and Barbro is drawn into telling him of the welcome prepared in Act I and the words of the ballad her father had taught her. They go, but Måns's original intention is fulfilled, and the King's conscience is stirred: 'Who sent them?' he asks, 'Here I, the highest of judges, sit on the bench of the accused'. This is the prelude to his acceptance of political compromise.

Chastisement is followed by mercy, a remission of sins and the joy of a second chance. Strindberg altered the facts of history to express this idea. There is historical evidence that Gustav, threatened in Stockholm by the approach of the rebels in 1544, summoned an army of Dalesmen to his aid. In the play, the King knows nothing about their coming; it may be another hostile force which is approaching, the final blow to his hopes. The feet are pounding the stairs, and the drunken, laughing, ebullient Engelbrekt, the skier out of his past life, is in the chamber, before Gustav is sure that the Dalesmen have come to prove their loyalty yet again and to help him put down the last rebellion of his reign. The invisible hand of providence, which kingship merely caricatures, has saved him and his Sweden again. The barbarous Norse god (a Wagnerian figure, perhaps) has given way to the ideal of the Christian monarch.

Erik XIV continues directly from *Gustav Vasa* (and the two have been combined in a single performance[7]). The continuity is emphasised by his use of the same setting for Act I of *Erik XIV* as for Act V of the previous play, and the motif of Gustav throwing his war hammer soon recurs, as Eric throws everything, nails as well as hammer, serving-basket and bed clothes. This crazy pantomime typifies a very differently conceived second play. Göran Persson, out of favour, turns Erik's anger by clowning, as he would tease a cross child into good humour. (Falstaff with Prince Hal has been identified as a model of their relationship.) The dialogue acknowledges the popular view of Göran as Erik's evil genius and his mistress (later Queen) Karin Månsdotter as his good angel, only to put this essentially medieval notion aside, for this is no morality play but a tragedy of character and the randomness of events. Terrible and touchingly gentle moments are thrown pell-mell together. This is one of the plays that introduce young children, confirming the nursery as metaphor for the reign. The King's attachment to his children is shown in the way he speaks and plays with them and even knows little Sigrid's dolls individually. 'Blind Paleface' is the worn toy Sigrid, unnoticed, wraps in the text of the speech Erik is supposed to make to the Estates, a small action that leads, within a single scene, to his retreat in confusion from the parliament chamber and then his distraught rush to join personally in the butchery of the lords held prisoner in the cellar. Thus, unspoiled by an explicit word, the playwright had identified Erik himself with the doll, a puppet moved by forces he does not perceive or understand.

On the day of his wedding to Karin, which Strindberg has also made the day of his deposition, Erik is haunted by awareness that it is Pentecost. The last scene of the play is based on Christ's parable of the kingdom of heaven as a marriage feast (St. Matthew, chapter 22): when the nobles invited to the banquet do not come, Erik orders the common people to be admitted. While they gorge themselves, and Karin's father, the stubbornly proud and puritanical Måns Knecht, brought round at last, plays the host, Erik and Göran sit apart, relaxed, with time now to talk of their lives, having accepted that their story is over. It is the counterpart of scenes in *To Damascus*: surreal, and among the models for the anarchic last supper in Buñuel's *Viridiana*. For Strindberg it represents a moment when the spiritual reality in history takes a preternaturally clear, visionary form.

When he published *The Swedish People* in 1882, Strindberg's critical estimate of Charles XII (1682–1718) aroused public protest. The prevalent nationalist view of this monarch was based substantially on the great military exploits of Charles's youth when he had repelled attacks made on Sweden by the Northern Alliance of Russia, Poland and Denmark. His death from a stray bullet before he reached the age of forty was the other essential ingredient in his legend. Strindberg chose to focus only on the King's last years, the period of defeat and retreat, and of economic disaster within a Sweden drained of wealth by long wars. He treats Charles as a representative of political absolutism in decline ('A strong will that struggles against the course of historical development') and introduces a dramatic link between the downward course of his career and the death of Louis XIV in France. By telescoping historical events, Strindberg composes a deliberately broken dramatic action which yet has a nagging tragic intensity. Particularly effective is his introduction of the persuasive rogue, Görtz, to be Charles's minister (in an episode which echoes Erik XIV's strengthening of his position by bringing in the able Göran to conduct his affairs), then moving directly to the failure of Görtz's policy, against all the conventions of dramatic plot which lead us to expect at least a high period of success.

Strindberg wrote with reference to *Charles XII* (in *Letters to the Intimate Theatre*): 'Every criminal has the right to defend himself, so I decided to plan my drama as a classical tragedy of fate and catastrophe'. The play does not explore the psychology of the 'criminal', or make a critical analysis of his military strategy or statecraft. It has been compared to a symphony in a minor key, and its principal theme is spiritual death. The King, a cold, withdrawn and ultimately pitiful figure, is only the chief of the walking dead who appear on stage. Strindberg uses a succession of devices to rob the character of colour and vitality: in Act I, he is sick, exhausted and voiceless, and only hoarse whispers come from him in the second Act, too; throughout Act III we wait for him to appear, as the figures on stage gather before a shuttered house and are rewarded only with the emergence of a lackey who lowers the flag to half-mast; in two scenes the actor has to play the role lying down on the camp bed which is this King's peculiar attribute, in contrast with the traditional stage throne.

Strindberg surrounds the monarch with his people: a considerable stage chorus deployed in *ensembles* to very different effect from the pageantry of *The Saga of the Folkungs*. The process starts in Act I, where the set and lighting have a formidable influence on mood: it is just before a chill, grey dawn on the edge of a dark sea; a burnt-out house, where a man in rags searches for traces of his former home and family (an image which becomes the basis of *The Burned House*), occupies the centre of the stage, with a view of other ruined buildings, and beside it stands an apple tree blown in the wind, stripped of most of its leaves and with a single fruit remaining at the top. A crowd of national councillors and representatives of the four estates comes to intercept the King when he lands from his ship and to lay their complaints before him. Strindberg's use of the ragged man and the coastguard to comment on the scene has the double effect of causing the larger groups to recede from us and, though individual figures have lines to speak, they remain close to anonymity and have some of the unreality of figures in a dumbshow. The general composition of the third Act is rather similar in that a small group is interposed between the audience and the rest of the scene: the ragged man from Act I, a character labelled the Malcontent, and the court Dwarf, a melancholy fool, who carries a violin and plays occasional snatches of an intensely sad Bach saraband at intervals through the play.

Emptiness and silence are twin main themes of this Act. Strindberg keeps dialogue minimal and centre stage unoccupied: groups of petitioners in a city square approach the house far back, at an angle to the backcloth, seeking the King, but are sent away. One persistent woman is given a voice only to be seen in the Man's appalled hallucination as the simulacrum of his dead wife. An episode in the previous act has already called into question the reality of the Man himself: he stands looking down on the King as though seeing a phantom on the bed, and the King stares back unsure whether this is a dream, while the intruder gives his name as Hunger, intensifying the horror of the moment. (It is the only name given him in the play.)

Act IV offers a contrast to the rest of the play in mood and tempo. Though the fact that this King was most at home on battlefields is remembered in the tent-shaped veranda of his house and the camp bed in the garden, his repressed sexuality is now the main theme. Strindberg indicates *'an old white statue of Venus'*, the tutelary genius of a scene which introduces the contrasted character of Swedenborg (here the self-confessed womaniser more than the mystic philosopher) with his sweetheart, Emerentia, who is determined to tempt the woman-hating King. Yet Charles repulses three women in turn, until, at the end of the act, the impression that the whole play presents a dead world is most powerfully created:

> (*Shabby-looking men and boys begin to gather by the wall at back. They appear silently . . . and sit there, one, two, three, but are not noticed yet by the people on the stage.*)
>
> GORTZ (*Uneasy*): Something is happening that makes me uneasy but I don't understand . . .
> KING: Do you see anything? I see nothing, but I hear this terrible silence!
> (trans. Walter Johnson, *Queen Christina* etc p. 157)[8]

The drama comes to its close in a night scene where Strindberg seems to be aiming at a Rembrandtesque chiaroscuro. Apart from the lantern in the foreground, areas of light suggest camp fires, torches and fitful gleams of moonlight from between scudding clouds. Part of a Norwegian fortress is seen in the background, providing a final symbol of death in its roof like *'a large, black sarcophagus'*. This and other omens are recognised in the dialogue, until the eerie climax of the lines: 'LEIF: Are you aware that we are talking as if he were dead?/SWEDENBORG: He *is* dead!' is followed by a flare and the report of a gun. Then cries out of the darkness and from different directions announce 'The king is shot!' (The mystery of who fired the shot is maintained, but the hint that the death was decreed 'in a higher court' is strongly conveyed.) After a few moments of confused words and movements, the stage is emptied of actors and is gradually taken over by blackness, as first the camp fires go out, then the torches and lantern are removed. Before the curtain falls, one further point of light comes up at the back: the lantern supposedly shining in the trench where the King's body has been found.

The play as a whole has the muted severity and meditative depth of a late Beethoven sonata, and in this way anticipates the chamber plays.

7
'The Dance of Death'

The Dance of Death has been one of Strindberg's most influential plays, a model for Sartre's *Huit Clos*, for O'Neill's *Long Day's Journey into Night* and Albee's *Who's Afraid of Virginia Woolf?* It has attracted many leading actors by the opportunity it gives for virtuoso performances.[1] Yet there has been more agreement about the power and originality of the work than on its interpretation.

Close links are evident between this play and the 'naturalistic' group, *The Father*, *Creditors* and even *Miss Julie*, in material and form. There are echoes of earlier situations in this presentation of a couple locked into a marriage of mutual torment, a see-sawing struggle for dominance, and a repetitive, cyclic action involving a triangle of two men and a woman. A major difference is in the nature of the setting: here, the staged room is in a fortress with huge double doors looking out on the shore where guns point out to sea; and a sentry, regularly marching past with sabre drawn, extends the symbolism and contributes to the rhythm of the play's opening. The couple, especially the Captain, are older and more aware of the imminence of death than the characters of the earlier plays. Indeed death, threatening annihilation to the self, is the principal force that the inhabitants of the fortress have armed themselves against, and the dance of the title takes stage form as a grotesquely defiant exhibition of vigour with strong sexual connotations. At Strindberg's own Intimate Theatre, August Falck, in full military rig, helmeted and brandishing his own sabre, gave a terrifying impression of ageing man defending himself against his final and most intimate enemy.

On the other hand, Part I of *The Dance of Death* opens with a dialogue of more thorough-going realism than those earlier plays can match. The prevailing tone varies between empty indifference and cynical acceptance – of an overwhelming tedium. Should a door be closed? What's for dinner? Has the post come? Such questions define the emptiness and purposelessness of the passing hours. What is there to think of but butcher's bills to be paid and domestic inconvenience? They might as well play cards. Everything is said, done and received with an air of long repetition, the absence of expectation of anything new and interesting to break the routine. Edgar (the Captain) and Alice, close to the date of their silver wedding, know each other far too well to have appearances to keep up, or to listen to each other with real attention. They exchange home truths and mouth old grievances with blunted feeling. Edgar is arrogant and Alice is vain. Both have fallen into the habit of bickering as the form their companionship takes. The sense of monotony is alleviated, and the action gets under way, with the arrival of an old associate (friend or enemy?), Alice's cousin Kurt. Left alone together again briefly, Edgar is roused to speculate to Alice, 'I wonder if everyone's life is like this', and they try to think of a happy family among their acquaintances.

Yet from the first moment the two characters suggest an extraordinary degree of vitality pent up within them, sensed from the sting of their remarks, the abundance of their disgust and an edge of cynical humour. It takes physical form in the first moment of surprise, when the play abandons the style of naturalism: as Alice sits at the piano and plays 'The Entry of the Boyars' in an accompaniment to the cossack dance (Edgar performs) to entertain their guest. He has a seizure while dancing, and the others think at first that he is dead. According to one theory, this *is* the moment of Edgar's death, and the strangeness of the rest of the play is explicable on the grounds that it is a Swedenborgian vision in which the Captain's ghost takes part, redeeming Kurt in particular by gradually taking the evil of the environment into his own person.[2] However, the text does not clearly confirm this view, and it would not be easy to convey it unambiguously to an uninitiated audience. The Captain's generalisation that 'All life is gruesome', taken together with Kurt's remark, near the end of Act I, that whenever he had quarrelled with Edgar 'his image took on strange forms and monstrous proportions', haunting his mind, gives a basis for another reading of the play, in both its parts, as a satire on life. The opposite of idealisation is such satire: a consistently negative view of human nature and circumstances, emphasising vices rather than virtues, corruption and ugliness rather than beauty and hope. 'Humanity is scum', the Captain's opinion, sums it up. Alice and Edgar measure their present existence against their false image of gaiety in the Copenhagen bar; they share no memories of young love like those of Adolf and Laura in *The Father*, for such mixed experience is alien to the nature of all but the end of Part I of *The Dance of Death*.

Strindberg does not deny the mixture of joy and pain, but isolates the opposed elements, presenting young love, its dreams and occasional joys among its cruelties, in the drama of the second generation, Judith and Allan, counterpointed to that of their parents, in Part II. Finally, the satirical vision is put in perspective by the surprising eulogy of Edgar, the idealised view, with which Part II ends: 'LIEUTENANT: Miss Judith's father was a good and noble man.' (trans. M. Meyer, II, 412). He repeats his judgment and draws Alice and Kurt into adding their tributes:

> ALICE: . . . My husband, the love of my youth – yes, laugh! – he *was* in spite of everything, a good and noble man.
> KURT: . . . He was brave too. The way he fought, for himself, and for others.

Hatred is at rest, though it can be remembered and acknowledged, and another image of Edgar presents itself to Alice:

> I've been seeing him, I see him now, as he was when he was twenty. I must have loved that man.
> (trans. M. Meyer, II, 463)

After the deadly, measured opening, there is a tremendous increase in the tempo of Part I. The characters assume a furious energy. The images they use in their speech and invoke in their actions become more gothic: Alice fantasises her life as that of a maiden imprisoned in a tower, and the Captain assigns himself the role of Bluebeard; images of demonic possession multiply, and the motif of vampirism becomes central, as it draws together their perceptions of the environment as hell and of evil as an infection carried by the kiss of lust. (For there is only lust, not love, only malice and jealousy, not magnanimity or forgiveness, in this hellish world.) Kurt is inevitably drawn in and made into a monster like the others; indeed it is he who responds to Alice's hideous challenge by giving the first vampire bite. Alice and Edgar, before his arrival, have recalled what has happened in the past when a third person has entered their lives. Thus Strindberg suggests that the play's action is only a fragment of a constantly repeating pattern, a slice of eternity; and the pattern is reinforced by the recurrences – sometimes only momentary – of coma, the condition of insensibility which seems like death or spiritual withdrawal to another plane of existence, which overtakes Edgar again and again. A similar nightmare effect, dislocating our normal sense of time, is achieved by the changes in Alice's appearance in Part I: from dark-haired in Act I to grey-haired in the first scene of Act II, then back to dark-haired in the second scene. The motif recurs early in Part II: Allan has seen an old photograph of his father (Kurt) with grey hair, on which the latter comments, 'Ten years ago I went grey-haired in a single night. Later it returned to its own colour. Of its own accord'. By such touches, here and in other plays, Strindberg disturbs belief that the universe his characters inhabit is ruled entirely by natural forces. In the midst of life they are in death, and death is a spiritual state governed by different laws.

The end of Part I is a return to realistic presentation of normality, but with a difference from the beginning. The grotesque events they have acted out seem to have invigorated Alice and Edgar. Certainly they are more cheerful and more reconciled to their situation – the human situation – and to each other. The problem now is 'How stupid life is . . . One used to fight, now one only shakes one's fists'. They agree to celebrate their silver wedding, something to look forward to: 'They'll laugh at us, but what of that?' Even hell, in Strindberg's depiction of it, is not absolute. Like Maurice, in *Crimes and Crimes*, the couple have awakened from a bad dream. Strindberg later summed up his view of the rhythm of life in the Note he added as a brief preface to *A Dream Play*:

> Sleep, the liberator, often seems a tormentor, but when the agony is harshest comes the awakening and reconciles the sufferer with reality – which, however painful, is yet a mercy, compared with the agony of the dream.
> (trans. M. Meyer, II, [553])

Edgar and Alice know that they will torment each other again and again, that the mood of hate, and the experience of the world that corresponds to it, will inevitably recur. In case Part I leaves us in doubt on that score, Part II illustrates the ingenious variations that are possible. The well-known critic, Northrop Frye, associates satire, in modern as well as ancient forms, with the experience of winter, in the mythological perception of life which arises from its seasonal pattern. Part I of *The Dance of Death* is altogether a winter play, but winter is contrasted with summer in Part II, and the effect is not simply testimony to love as well as hate, painful joy as well as gleeful fury, in the spectrum of human emotions; the hopefulness of youth, reflected in the white and gold setting of Kurt's drawing-room, with the garden in bloom outside the windows, and enacted in the escape of the young lovers from the island, looks back as well as forward: to a phase of life their parents knew and have forgotten, and to the darker phase that they themselves can surely not escape. The young girl is called Judith, and Alice seizes on the name in order to identify Edgar with Holofernes and his daughter's defiance of his authority as the vengeful, murderous triumph of the female over the

1. August Strindberg with his daughters, Karin and Greta, in Switzerland, 1886.
Pre-set exposure by Strindberg himself.

2. August Strindberg, 'The City', painted between 1900 and 1907.

3. Robert Loraine in *The Father*, directed by Milton Rosmer, Everyman and Apollo Theatres, 1927. This is the same moment from the play as shown below.

4. Wilfred Lawson in *The Father*, directed by Peter Cotes, Arts Theatre, 1953.

5. Beatrix Lehmann as Laura in *The Father*, Arts Theatre, 1953.

6. *To Damascus*, directed by Ingmar Berman, Royal Dramatic Theatre, Stockholm, 1974. With Jan-Olof Strandberg as the Unknown, right foreground.

7. *Crimes and Crimes (Brott och Brott)*, Royal Dramatic Theatre, Stockholm, 1900. Augusta Lindberg as Henriette, August Palme as Maurice.

8. Harriet Bosse as Henriette, Uno Henning as Maurice, in *Crimes and Crimes*, directed by Alf Sjöberg, Royal Dramatic Theatre, Stockholm, 1936.

9. *Charles XII/Karl XII*, with August Palme as the King, Royal Dramatic Theatre, Stockholm, 1902.

10. *Gustav Vasa*, Göteberg City Theatre, 1934, directed by Knut Ström, with Sven Miliander as Göran and Georg Rydeberg as Prince Erik.

11. *The Pelican* at Strindberg's Intimate Theatre, Stockholm, 1907-10.
August Falck, as the Son, is on the left by the table, and Manda Björling, as the Daughter, is seated on the right.

12. The art nouveau design for *Swanwhite* at the Intimate Theatre. The set based on this was eventually abandoned and curtains were used instead.

13. Olof Molander's production of *Ghost Sonata*, at the Royal Dramatic Theatre, Stockholm, 1962.

14. *A Dream Play*, produced by Victor Castegren, Svenska Theatre, Stockholm, 1907, with Harriet Bosse as Indra's Daughter.

15. Max von Sydow as the Stranger in Strindberg's *The Burned House* (*Brända tomten*), directed by Alf Sjöberg, at the Royal Dramatic Theatre, Stockholm, 1970.

male. It is she, the mother, who remains to exult, when Edgar suffers his fatal stroke, and symbolically enacts her image of the beheading of the tyrant. The monstrous animal imagery traditional to satire becomes part of a scene which must recall to theatre-goers the blinding of Gloucester in *King Lear* (and Edward Bond's encapsulation of the Senecan horrors of our modern world in his play, *Lear*):

> THE CAPTAIN: *speechless, spits in her face.*
> ALICE: If you can still spit venom, viper, I'll tear the tongue out of your throat.
> *She gives him a blow on the ear.*
> The head is off . . . If you have any more heads, hydra, we'll take them too!
> *She pulls his beard.*
> So there is justice on earth after all!
> (trans. Elizabeth Sprigge *Five Plays* p. 231)

The objectivity of naturalism survives in Strindberg's presentation of the extremes to which both husband and wife are compulsively driven in their deadly battle. The play does not allow continuing sympathy or continuing condemnation of either character, and the didactic element, clearly pointing out sins and a way of repentance, in *Crimes and Crimes* and *Easter*, is overwhelmed in *The Dance of Death* by the fatalism in its imagery of eternal recurrence. If the play is strangely exhilarating rather than depressing, this owes less to the calm of the final moments, with the return of the ideal image and a kind of forgiveness, than to the fact that the characters appear in their element in the hell they are programmed to create, entering wholeheartedly and vigorously into the horrid dance ('getting old . . . isn't nice, but it's interesting'). 'Perhaps we're a bit like that ourselves'.

The interweaving, development and recapitulation of themes and motifs on analogy with musical composition, is perceptible in *The Dance of Death* through its organisation into distinct movements, each clearly defined by a dominant emotion, and contributes to the fatalistic effect. For this form does not seem to arise out of the actions and decisions of the individual characters. They themselves are contained and controlled by the pattern they do not will. In this respect, Symbolism, as a movement in the arts which cultivated the abstract, purely aesthetic qualities of music in all the media of expression, leaned towards pessimism and turned away from purposive social battles towards contemplation. Such is the mood and posture of *A Dream Play*, which came to be Strindberg's own favourite work and the one which has most lured and tantalised stage directors.

8
Towards Total Theatre: 'A Dream Play'

Strindberg acknowledged Maeterlinck's influence on his peasant play, *The Crown Bride*, and on *A Dream Play*. In a third work, *Swanwhite*, he created an example of the same genre as Maeterlinck's *The Blue Bird* and its sequel, *The Betrothal*, but antedating them. This was one of his most popular plays, a fairytale piece, half-intended for children, like the earlier *Lucky Peter's Travels* and *The Keys of the Kingdom*. Unlike the realistically framed *Blue Bird*, it is not technically a dream play, but is set entirely in a fairytale palace (for which young Knut Ström designed a charming *art nouveau* set). Its young lovers are hardly more than children; indeed it is the resolution of the relationship between Swanwhite and the mother image, split between stepmother and guardian angel, which has to be achieved before her love of the Prince can be fulfilled. The elegance of the play's structure and stagecraft goes far to guard against sentimentality. 'Eros is not the main theme', explained Strindberg to Anna Flygare, who was to play Swanwhite, 'the symbolism relates to Caritas, the great love which suffers everything, forgives, hopes, and believes, however much it is betrayed. This is illustrated by the Stepmother's change of character, but most of all by the final scene: love is stronger than death'.[1] The comment underlines the thematic parallel with Maeterlinck's plays of death and love. Sibelius wrote music for *Swanwhite* in 1907, though his later adaptation of it into an orchestral suite is rather better known than the original score. Robert Layton has said of it, 'More praised than played . . . It makes a very considerable impact when heard in the context of Strindberg's play'.[2]

There are dark elements in *Swanwhite*; *The Crown Bride* is altogether darker and continues in a new vein the Christian treatment of guilt and remorse from *Advent* and *Easter*. The heroine, Kersti, is a peasant Lady Macbeth, who will murder her own child to obtain her crown, drawing her lover, the weaker, 'good' Mats, after her.[3] Critics have written of the medieval quality of the play, but its actual period is the second half of the nineteenth century. Thus, if we seek analogies in the drama of other countries, Spain perhaps provides the closest, in Lorca's *Blood Wedding*. In style it is half-way to folk opera: the dialogue is formally patterned, sometimes in antiphonal passages; Strindberg's directions require the careful, musical orchestration of sound effects; folk songs are included and, cutting across them, he introduced the key melodic line of the play in the Neckan's (or river sprite's) repeated *leitmotiv*, 'I hope, I hope that my Redeemer liveth'. (He himself provided the music for the Neckan's song, after failing to discover how the fiddle accompaniment was traditionally played.)

In the writing of *The Crown Bride*, Strindberg seems to

have drawn on long buried feelings for the death of his first child in early infancy. His love of rural Sweden emerges through a poetry of landscape and seasons threaded through with images of the natural opposites of fire and water, light and dark, love and hate. In the world it conjures up, animistic belief lives side-by-side with Christian faith, a fitting environment for a spiritual growth in Kersti which begins with her violation of nature and continues through the reassertion of natural feelings within her. Ingmar Bergman produced the play on a bare stage at Malmö, in 1952, to astonishing effect at the end, when the submerged church rises in a vision out of the flood waters, 'Using only lighting and screening effects to suggest the dark perilous wastes of a frozen ocean that fade away into pitch darkness'.[4]

There are several strata of composition discernible in *A Dream Play*. While working on it, Strindberg used three different titles, suggesting multiple themes: *Prisoners*, *The Corridor Drama* and *The Growing Castle*.[5] Indeed, he seems to have brought together at least two distinctly conceived, separate compositions. The scenes in the finished work which are set in a backstage area of a theatre correspond to the first of these; the second composition focuses on the image of the fairytale castle and is used to frame the succession of dreams which make up the rest of the play.

A Dream Play was completed in its original form in 1901. Strindberg was excited by parallels he could now see between the work he had created and concepts of oriental mystical religion, especially Buddhism. So he introduced changes in the text to turn what had been unconscious, latent meanings into explicit references. He completed the process, and radically altered the balance of his play, by adding a Prologue in 1906 in anticipation of the first production at the Svenska Theatre, the following year. (Having been regarded up to that time as unstageable, the work had a great and surprising success.) Strindberg's Prologue was modelled on Goethe's Prologue in Heaven for Part I of *Faust*.[6] It takes the form of a verse dialogue between the God Indra and his Daughter (God in two persons, male and female) as they look down on the planet Earth. Her father sends her down among humanity, as in Christian tradition God sent his Son. The playwright's immediate concern, in making this addition, may have been to reassure his audience, giving them a familiar point of reference to make acceptance of his new dramatic techniques rather easier; it is an assurance of the author's authority, his control over the work, a pledge of its coherence and an expression of detachment from it.

Ingmar Bergman's adaptation of *A Dream Play*, seen in London and in Edinburgh in the 1970s and published in Michael Meyer's translation, cuts out most of the Prologue, but leaves enough still to give a doctrinal rationalisation to what follows. An adaptation which omitted the Prologue entirely would show more clearly that the play Strindberg originally wrote was a work for the twentieth century rather than the nineteenth. It plunges us into an unpredictable and unstable world, with no exposition, no careful identification of characters, and it proceeds against logic. The spectators are given no advantage over the characters on stage, but have to take the play on its own terms, as it unfolds, go with its drift and make of it what they can. At a climax in the action a door is ritually opened to reveal the secret of life; but there is nothing behind it. This emblem of the philosophical Absurd matches the general method of the play but conflicts with the Prologue.

The opening of *A Dream Play* is Alice in Wonderland

stuff, absurd in the popular sense of the word. Against a backcloth painted with gigantic hollyhocks, surrounding a castle with a gilded dome crowned by a chrysanthemum in bud,[7] a daughter asks her father how much growth the building has made in a year. This is the Daughter of the Prologue, but she is not immediately given the status of a Daughter of God; indeed, who she is remains ambiguous through the whole of the play (like Balzac's Séraphita who takes human form as Swedenborg's niece): not just Everywoman, not a redeemer, but a sympathetic observer suddenly entrapped in the action; it is possible to see her as an *anima* figure. Her pilgrimage through the world gives the play its thread of continuity, but she starts out as Agnes, the Glazier's child. Like an actor who does not know his lines, the Glazier registers bewilderment at her question but quickly picks up his cue and improvises a fantasy which overtops hers:

> it has grown eight feet, but that's because they've manured it. And . . . you'll see that a wing has grown on the side facing the sun.
>
> (trans. M. Meyer II, p. 564)

Even physical perspectives are ambiguous: played as she must be by an adult actress, the Daughter's height is incongruously close to the Glazier's but dwarfed by the forest of hollyhocks. Her whim is to enter the painted castle, surely to find a prisoner there to whose rescue she can come like a good fairy; and the drama moves with her thought. The Officer, discovered seated in a bare room, behaves like a small boy in a soldier suit, banging his toy sword on the table; and his complaint of injustice is answered in a flashback (or forward?) to a scene with his father and mother which reminds him that he hid away a copy of *Swiss Family Robinson* (not *Alice in Wonderland*!) and let his brother be blamed for losing it. It may be relevant that the book is one in which children take on grown-up roles. For these introductory scenes both establish an image of men and women as children in understanding, and display characters in which memory and the child's consciousness remain active constituents of adult personality. (The Billsticker's tragi-comedy lies in his disappointment that the fishing net, which absorbed his childish desires, makes so little difference to his adult self.) Hence the constant variations of tone between childish curiosity or moodiness and adult longing or anguish.

In this opening, with a light touch, Strindberg puts his audience in a frame of mind to accept a free play of fantasy, drift with the dream of consciousness and be receptive to the changes of mood, as in listening to music. There follows, instead of the development of a particular situation in a regular dramatic plot, a kaleidoscope of many characters, in numerous settings, clearly defined but briefly glimpsed, with their separate stories compressed into motifs. Realism is transcended in the presentation of snatches from everyday life as part of a universal panorama, with a fluidity quite alien to the medieval cosmic pageants it recalls in some ways. *A Dream Play*, in the words of Anton Kaes, is 'deeply rooted in the tradition of symbolist aesthetics': it pursues the essence of human experience and attempts to communicate it directly, bypassing the intellect and the separate senses through a synthesis of different arts. Strindberg's form of total theatre is quite distinct from that of Wagner (whose work he hated). Whereas Wagner used mythic story as a traditional means of holding audience attention and *leitmotiv* structure to bring conceptual values into music, Strindberg dissolves logic and narrative plot into an approximation to symphonic form.[8] (What James Joyce did to the novel, in *Ulysses*, is the obvious parallel.) Conflict, which had given his naturalistic plays their dynamism, is only occasional and incidental in *A Dream Play*, and this remains true of the last phase of his work, the chamber plays he wrote for his Intimate Theatre. The clashes seem like echoes from old battles, final spasms from a dying impulse. The energy is now diffused through very different dramatic rhythms. In place of intense excitement, *A Dream Play* induces a more contemplative response with its own kind of depth.

Its considerable range includes contradictory attitudes, as well as antithetical emotions, joy and grief, hope and disillusionment, love, envy, celebration, rejection. Although the prevailing sense of life it conveys is pessimistic – compassion is the only resolution of mankind's painful destiny which is offered –, satire is not absent, and the Coalheavers' view of the golden life of Fairhaven expresses a radical determination, 'It's time to bring out the knives and operate on this rotten body'; the Lawyer caps his own observation that 'All reformers end in prison or the madhouse' with the thought that it is the respectable who put them in prison, while what puts them in the madhouse is their own despair at the hopelessness of the struggle. As in *To Damascus*, but with accelerating tempo, the play moves into reverse at the climax, finding its way back through successive scenes to the growing castle again, while characters, moods and motifs are gathered into a recapitulation which brings not only repetition but understanding.

In the manuscript and first edition of the play the text is divided into three movements marked by roman numerals. Another structural division overlaps with this, though it also takes a triple form: the three chief male characters, the Officer, the Lawyer and the Poet, are successive companions of the Daughter in different stages of her pilgrimage.

(The fact that she starts out with the Glazier has commonly been ignored.) Some productions have gone so far as to cast a single actor in the three roles, thus strengthening the suggestion that they represent three aspects of man, or three approaches to life: perhaps the active way of the common man (the Officer is also schoolboy, lover and schoolmaster); the way of affliction through the conviction of sins and pursuit of justice and atonement (the Lawyer, having been burdened with mankind's dreadful confessions, is treated as a scapegoat and crowned with thorns instead of laurels); and the visionary way of the Poet. These are not separately confined to the three movements. The Officer appears more frequently than the others, in a variety of episodes; the dramatic core of the play, where it comes nearest to the intensity of psychological realism, is the rejection of the Lawyer in the solemn graduation ceremony and its sequence in a compressed ordeal of marriage between the Lawyer and the Daughter; but the thematic structure has a different centre – in the Fingal's Cave scene where the general movement of the play goes into reverse and this is marked by the repetition in variant form of a brief stichomythic dialogue between Daughter and Poet on the relationship of poetry to reality and dream. This dialogue claims the supremacy of the Poet's vocation, and Bergman's adaptation of the play, which locates the whole drama in the Poet's consciousness, is in accord with it, though it goes further in giving Strindberg's face to the generalised figure. Yet there are rival themes. Poetry itself is incidental to the theme of vision signalled at the start by the Glazier with his diamond (later used to open the door on mystery) and most fully developed in the dialogue when the Blind Man tells his anecdote of the child's answer to 'Why do people cry when they are sad?' – 'because their eyes have to be washed sometimes so that they can see more clearly'. This theme is negatively counterbalanced by the visual motif of Christine pasting up the windows of the Lawyer's room. It is intersected by a line which re-echoes in identical form through the play, 'Men are to be pitied' (Elizabeth Sprigge notes that the idiomatic 'It's a shame about people' catches the tone of the original more nearly).[9] By the variety of patterning he has introduced, Strindberg has made the play resistant to a single, dogmatic interpretation. His close interweaving of themes, like the iterative imagery in Shakespeare's plays, suggests lines for the imagination to follow.

He acknowledged his debt to Maeterlinck (then the leading symbolist playwright and spokesman for the paradoxical concept of static drama) in the brief prefatory note first published with Edwin Björkman's translation of *A Dream Play* into English. He made notes for further prefatory paragraphs which would also refer to Shakespeare's *The Tempest* and Calderon's *La Vida es Sueño* (*Life's a Dream*) as forerunners of his view of the world as illusion. In retrospect, critics have preferred to suggest connections with Freud's *Interpretation of Dreams*, claiming priority in dream symbolism for the playwright who had independently followed the researches and theories of some of Freud's masters, including Maudsley and Charcot. Strindberg had commented on his friend Munch's addiction to symbols of male sexuality and is unlikely to have been blind to the symbolism of male potency in the growing castle which, at the end, is consumed in flames, as the bud which crowns it opens into full blossom. Nor is such a recognition likely to have disturbed the author who wrote the seduction scene in *Miss Julie.* The settings of *A Dream Play* are drawn partly from everyday life, partly from the landscapes and seascapes already established in Strindberg's imagination and which also appear in his paintings on wood and canvas. Fingal's Cave (the grotto where the organ plays and which opens on to the sea), symbolically antithetical to the growing castle, corresponds to a series of 'wonderland' pictures.[10] In notes on his paintings, Strindberg emphasised the multiplicity of meanings they could suggest, and the whole technique of *A Dream Play* – from the initial bringing together of corridor drama and growing castle – resists too exhaustive and systematic an analysis, however skilful. Escape from logic and what William Blake termed 'single vision' into an expanding universe and an inexhaustible life of imagination and spirit is the achievement Strindberg has pioneered.

The play routs the notion that a dramatist's business is confined to the writing of dialogue. The always perverse attempt to separate the play as literature from the total dramatic creation is impossible with this work. This period saw the emergence of the director in the theatre, and Strindberg, whose theatrical interests were as alive as his literary talents, accepted a director's responsibilities as part of the dramatist's task, never forgetting that performance alone completes the play and determined that all aspects of the staging should extend the play's expressiveness in the liveliest, yet totally unified way.

He himself realised that the play was open to production in quite contrary ways. All the available resources of theatrical machinery, together with the infinite possibilities of modern lighting, could be pressed into service to create the magic of constantly shifting stage illusion, a kaleidoscope of ravishing 'effects' following, in Scandinavia, the tradition of Hans Christian Andersen's fairytale theatre. Alternatively, Strindberg's later pursuit of a less obvious beauty through 'de-materialisation' points the way firmly to the Brechtian style of presentation now ubiquitous in 'alternative' theatre. It is clear from the text of *A Dream Play* that scene need not follow scene through a series of filmic dissolves. A very few simple properties adaptably used are enough: the tree without leaves becomes a hatstand for an indoor scene, and, when the hatstand functions as a candelabrum, the corridor is transformed into a great church. Yuri Lyubimov's splendid production of *Crime and Punishment* in London in 1983, dispensed with any kind of set or decor but made maximum dramatic use of a single property: a door moved easily about the stage as a convenience for the actors who, with an effect of improvisation, could use it to establish a variety of particular scenes. The modern origin of such procedure lies in the four-leaved-clover door of *A Dream Play*.

Inevitably, the object isolated from any pictorially realistic set acquires the force of a symbol, susceptible though it is to transformations. Strindberg's drama of the stage door makes only an oblique approach to the ancient metaphor of the world as theatre, yet he supplies crucial perspectives on life in the directest possible way. The fleetingness of life is made visible in the fall of leaves from the tree and the changed appearance of the Officer on each successive entrance in the first part of the play: as he grows dustier, his hair turns to grey, and the roses he carries wilt until only the dead stems are left. Then subjectivity has its revenge, using theatrical illusion to demonstrate the illusory nature of the forms life takes. The rhythm of the passage of time is *created*, as sun and moon, day and night are at command in a theatrical performance:

> *The lights come and go like a lighthouse beam . . .*
> OFFICER: *Speaking in time with the flashes.* Light and darkness; light and darkness.

DAUGHTER: *with the same timing.* Day and night; day and night. A merciful providence wants to shorten your waiting.

(trans. Elizabeth Sprigge, *Six Plays*, p. 209)

The acting of *A Dream Play* raises its own particular problems. A lyrical, predominantly melancholy performance can be given by players who accept the limited dramatic function of soloists and chorus in a concert performance under a strong conductor. Such an approach may produce an interesting and even moving effect, somewhere between drama and music, in which the usual energies of drama are subdued. An example, admittedly extreme, was given by the Canadian company, which presented Jean Herbier's version of *A Dream Play* spoken by actors who stood in oriental-style costumes against black velvet curtains, holding and manipulating puppets which represented Strindberg's characters, at the Edinburgh Festival of 1980. The performance was closer to the spirit of Maeterlinck's little plays for marionettes than to Strindberg. For anything like the full and various flavour of the play to come through, a gallery of cameo performances is required from the actors – concentrated acting which is able to convey idiosyncrasy, force and emotional depth in minutes, or even seconds, on stage. Only if it is as much a symphony of human experience and adventure as of sound and spectacle does the achievement of *A Dream Play*, in opening up new, major roads for twentieth-century drama, become evident.

It has sometimes been remarked that, in *A Dream Play*, Strindberg was moving towards the possibilities of the new medium of film, and Elizabeth Sprigge and others have deplored film-makers' neglect of this work. Ingmar Bergman has shown a truer appreciation of what the dramatist was doing. For, though Bergman's films are saturated with his knowledge of Strindberg's work, his productions of the plays have been confined to the theatre. The sense of strangeness and disorientation, as though the familiar world was breaking down under the assault of previously hidden forces, is even stronger in the later play, *Ghost Sonata*, but in all the post-Inferno drama it is largely conveyed by the strains put on the theatrical medium and the gaps that open up when it is forced beyond its normally recognised technical limits.

9
The Chamber Plays

The final development in Strindberg's art as a dramatist came about in the group of plays he wrote specifically for the repertoire of his Intimate Theatre: *Storm, The Burned House, Ghost Sonata, The Pelican* and a Christmas piece, *The Black Glove*. In calling them chamber plays, he associated his and Falck's theatre project with Max Reinhardt's contemporary opening of the Kammer-spielhaus (chamber playhouse) in Berlin, as well as suggesting that these works have a dramatic equivalence to chamber music. Although only *Ghost Sonata* declares in its title the symbolist cultivation of musical form, Strindberg referred to the whole group as his late sonatas, perhaps inviting comparison with those of Beethoven.

In some respects they are more obviously designed for a repertory company than for a studio theatre. They call for unexpectedly large casts, despite their otherwise concentrated quality, and require careful direction of the whole rather than a focus on one or two star roles. Furthermore, their settings offer problems for a small stage which demand imaginative solutions; indeed, they were hardly solved at Intiman, though hindsight persuaded Strindberg that radically simplified staging might hold the answer. One of his declared intentions, at the opening of the little theatre, was to challenge the substitution of length for intensity in the fashionable programmes of the day. (He was sympathetic to the good bourgeois couples who wanted to get home to bed at a reasonable hour.) The chamber plays are shorter than the usual three-act play, but sufficiently demanding of audience attention and response to occupy the whole of an evening's bill without short-changing their patrons. To the actors in the company he explained his concept of a drama constructed on the basis of a single strong theme, which the playwright could choose to treat in any way he wished, without regard for theatrical custom and convention, but only for a unity of form and style with his central idea.[1]

Written close together in time, it is not surprising that the chamber plays are interlinked by a number of images and themes which find their way into two or more of the individual works. The house of intertwined human destinies is chief of these. Hardly less significant are the motifs of consuming fire, the child lost and found, the return of the past in the present and the vampire (or evil mother) who drains the strength which should be nourished. Consequently, seeing or reading them together extends the implications of each. The everyday world is realistically evoked in the whole group of plays, only to be rendered transparent and astonishing under the pressure of a greater reality.

On the other hand, the diversity of the group is considerable. Except for *Ghost Sonata* and *The Black Glove*, the plays seem quite close to conventional realism, a reversion to the kinds of drama Strindberg was writing before *To*

Damascus. Yet there are subtle differences. Though *Storm* contains elements of an intrigue plot, this is not the skeleton of the play so much as the material around which emotions gather. The mood is predominantly elegiac, and the incidental dramatic climaxes emphasise by contrast the prevailing quietness which deepens at the end of the play. Strindberg suggests a passage from late summer to autumn and the verge of winter in human life, as natural as in the seasons of the year; the stirrings of a hope which had seemed dead, promising an Indian summer, broken up by stormy disturbances; and then an ebbing of the turbulent forces to leave resignation, final acceptance of the more withdrawn, solitary life of age. Such is the experience of the Master whose (younger) divorced wife and their child come back briefly, into his orbit, and involve him in their troubles, particularly the abduction of the child by her stepfather. When the dangers pass, they move on, out of his life again. The episode has brought a degree of reconciliation, but for the Master there is a sense of finality in this new peace. The familiar quality of the setting, in the residential area of a city during days of thunderous heat when most of the inhabitants seem to have fled into the country, contributes to the general mood: the low-temperature ordinariness of life in the street, the comings and goings of the postman, tradespeople, the casual visitor dropping in, the lamplighter as evening approaches, none of this is dispelled, but rather seen with abnormal clarity in silent flashes of lightning and atmospheric tension.

The Burned House,[2] by contrast, is rich in sardonic humour, unexpectedly associated with another elderly figure exploring his past. Having returned after many years abroad, he finds that the house where he spent his youth has just been burnt down – a case of arson, which brings in a detective and a host of suspects. Our visitor from far away to the country of the past probes the ruins, pieces together the story of the fire in conversation with the neighbourhood and ultimately discovers that the crime was committed by his own brother whose hopes of the insurance money are cheated through the chance of an unposted letter. So the play reaches a wryly happy ending for everyone. The set is transformed to suggest a glimpse of paradise restored. Even the guilty man is encouraged to face the future with the thought that his unenviable condition may bring him friends, while work is good for the character. The translators of this play have faced a considerable challenge to catch something of the salty colloquialism of Strindberg's dialogue which does much to anchor the play in the world we know.

Though he is, like the Master in *Storm*, making his own settlement with the past, the Stranger of *The Burned House* shows a quality of detachment, of almost academic interest in persons and events. He does not deny, nor require to be taken too seriously the rumours that he has second sight and that he has been 'over the river' of death, which are tokens of his detachment. Strindberg, in fact, uses this character as an authorial ambassador to show human life, its falsehood and truth, to the audience. The old man, Hummel, in *Ghost Sonata*, seems in the first scene to have a similar role and, like the Stranger, he also takes a benevolent interest in the fortunes of a Student. Yet Strindberg turns Hummel into a much more ambiguous figure: his benevolence and even his humanity are called gravely into question. From being the interpreter who controls the action in the interests of what he has to teach he changes into the accused – and condemned.

The Pelican is the tragedy in the group, a modern version of the *Choephori*, the middle play in Æschylus's Oresteian trilogy. Once more, as in *The Father*, Strindberg derived from his Greek model a basic, or archetypal, pattern of human relationships, the skull he saw beneath the skin of family life in his own day. The result is a bleak and horrifying view of the family, close in theme and some of its particulars to the equally horrifying, but in execution more ordinary *Mother-Love* which he had written in 1892. The Mother, in *The Pelican*, is a grasping and egotistical character who might have been created by Zola. The title ironically measures the distance between the tyranny she exerts over her son and daughter and the ideal of motherhood traditionally emblematised in the bird which, according to fable, draws its own blood to feed its young. Like Clytemnestra she is a widow, hiding a secret guilt for treachery (not in this instance actual murder) towards her late husband. There is no Ægisthus in the modern play, but part of his function – as Clytemnestra's lover – is transferred to the son-in-law, whose sexual interests and affections the mother prises away from her own daughter and attempts to draw towards herself. Strindberg's naturalistic understanding of how a self-confident ascendancy drains the will from its victims shows here in his presentation of the weakness and near-helplessness of the daughter and son, the source of the play's nightmarish atmosphere. Unlike Elektra and Orestes, they do not survive their revenge, but perish themselves in the fire, more a spiritual than a physical element, which consumes the whole house of misery. In their shared death, brother and sister regress to childhood in what is possibly a memory, but more probably a dream, of a summer picnic expedition to a beautiful island in which they share happiness with their father and, in the last moments of their consciousness, with their mother too – the good mother restored to them. The influence of Edgar Allan Poe, marked when Strindberg was writing his plays of hypnotism, *Pariah, Simoon*, even

Creditors, was still operative in the late plays, not least in the eerie and sinister mood established by the simple phenomena of sudden gusts of wind, banging doors and, above all, the movements of the empty rocking chair. These are not used like the familiar gothic trimmings of a tale to thrill audiences with sheer sensation: not the signs, but the mother's superstitious and fearful interpretation of them, through a malignancy of conscience, is the chilling factor.

The Black Glove, written as a Christmas play for the Intimate Theatre two years after the others in this group, has commonly been judged a slighter, less compelling piece of work altogether, perhaps an inevitable consequence of the practical intention with which Strindberg wrote it. Like *Storm* and *Ghost Sonata*, this too has a modern apartment-house setting, but the intersection of actuality with a dream action, in which terrible things happen only to be cancelled out when the warning is taken, seems more like a dramatic device – the dream itself is less disturbing as it is less compellingly vivid – than in *Crimes and Crimes*. The black glove itself is an obviously symbolic property: when it is lost, the nightmare starts, and the winning-through of human kindliness particularly in the young mother, Mrs Hard, is marked by the return of the glove to its human owner. Age, in the figure of an old man, is one of the themes interlinked in this last of the chamber plays as in its predecessors: here the restoration of the sick child is counterbalanced by the old man's peaceful death.

At the start of *Ghost Sonata* it is evident that Strindberg's interest in the inclusion of mime sequences, in *Miss Julie*, has taken a new turn. Before the dialogue launches into any exposition of the dramatic situation, *Ghost Sonata* offers a practical demonstration of the 'laws' governing its stage world. Strindberg's initial directions are specific about the placing of his characters at the rise of the curtain, allowing for some differences of level: where they are in relation to each other and when and how they move are matters as essential as in the choreography of a ballet; the dramatist presents his characters now, not primarily as psychologically defined individuals whose nature is revealed largely through dialogue, but as three-dimensional forms occupying and moving through space. The familiar metaphor of the play as a two-dimensional picture in its proscenium frame is inappropriate to this kind of stage work, which has more in common with sculpture, static and mobile.

The technique is close to the emphasis on the values of form and colour in contemporary abstract art. The spectator's eye is invited to relate the figure of the woman in black standing motionless on the stairs to the moving figure at the door, a woman engaged in commonplace chores; our nerves and muscles feel sympathetically the tug of contrary kinds of force in the stillness of the first and the rhythmical movements of the second, sweeping figure. The sense of the human body as a machine under the control of a will may be activated when its 'natural' movements are contrasted with the movement of the figure in a wheel chair, soon to be propelled to different stage positions by an attendant. (Samuel Beckett's explicit denials of influence from this play do nothing to weaken the observation that *Ghost Sonata* occupies an intermediate position between Maeterlinck's explorations of stage space, in *The Seven Princesses*, for instance, and Beckett's in *Endgame.*) For some long moments the audience has nothing to do but gaze and hear the sounds, especially bells, which suggest a city at leisure. There is no focal point, and a delay before the entrance which initiates the plot.

The first incident of the Milkmaid entering to tidy and refresh herself at the fountain is itself a dumbshow; and she continues to mime her response when the Student follows and speaks to her. This isolation of different human functions, corresponding to different senses, takes on metaphysical value, especially when Old Hummel in the wheelchair indicates that he can hear the Student but not see the Milkmaid. The figures peopling the stage are not all, it seems, on the same plane of being. As for the unusual extent to which the author demonstrates his control over them, the degree of independence he gives them as fully imagined characters, with past histories and present desires, is carefully counterpoised by reminders that they are images, puppets, in this play of his composing.

Instead of giving the Student a normal exit, when plot-development requires it, Strindberg encloses him in a box in full view of the audience. Certainly the box has the realistic and very up-to-date form of a telephone kiosk, but the style of the play gives every stage movement intrinsic significance and also endows every object it indicates with symbolic status. Like the telephone in *Easter*, or the telegraph in *Dance of Death*, this telephone is a meeting-point of modern science and the occult. The world of the play is one in which second sight operates to reveal what is normally hidden from human eyes; but it is also the world known to modern physics, with many dimensions beyond direct human perception and a space-time continuum which defies commonsense.

Though some of the most famous productions of the play have not exploited the possibility, Strindberg's directions for staging allow for distortion in the perspectives. (Artaud's projected design would have made the most of the opportunity.)[3] In the first scene, a *corner* of the fashionable Stockholm apartment house is to be shown, in the foreground a street, with another street leading off at an angle. The second and third scenes are within the house, scene ii focusing on the reception room, but the perspective is extended to show a section of the entrance hall and a further room, profusely decorated with hyacinths, set back and at an angle from the main stage area. In scene iii these arrangements are reversed, with the hyacinth room now centre stage. Strindberg operates a form of visual counterpoint between the separately defined areas in scenes ii and iii: as the players in the main area act out their scene, the spectator's eye has continually in view a second, undeveloped scene, its characters immobile, in the remoter area. No conventional plot development, no process of cause and effect, links scene iii in logical sequence to scene ii. On the contrary, the possibility is signalled and left inconclusive that the play gives in sequence two actions which would be simultaneous in actual time. What in the 'musical' pattern of the play is the recapitulation at the end of scene iii of the Student's song, first heard at the end of scene ii, may also confirm the idea that a single period of time has been artificially split and is now restored to unity for the final moments of the play.

An unusual deployment of dramatic conventions can be as disturbing as tricks unexpectedly played by one's own mind. Hints that time may move in different directions, that it may be cyclic, not serial, contribute to the eeriness of the experience *Ghost Sonata* offers, and the free intermixture of realism of detail with symbolism strengthens the effect. The first scene can be vividly evocative of an actual Sunday morning in Stockholm with newspapers and playbills enhancing the sense of immediacy, as the telephone box connects the stage with the city around the theatre; yet the house observed and described by 'Boss' Hummel to the Student is obviously a symbolic structure, at once real and unreal. The story of the previous night emerges, when a house collapsed and the Student worked to salvage the victims; and a further twist is his account of the strange, premonitory episode in which he caught up a child just *before* the collapse of the house – only to find his arms empty. What follows, in scene ii, is the fall of a house in the metaphoric sense: the same house? In scene iii, the innocent, ideal figure of the girl the Student's love claims wilts and vanishes behind the oriental death screen: an alternative way of expressing the same meaning as the anecdote of the phantom child? There is also a curious half-resemblance between what we learn, in scene i, of Hummel's former relationship with the Student's father and Hummel's present behaviour and the plan he carries on into scene ii.

By such means Strindberg communicates a sense of complex mysteries and hidden meanings to be fragmentarily glimpsed, but not explained away. He tempts the audience towards speculation, interpretation, but also controls and checks intellectual analysis by the evident aesthetic patterning of the play as a work of art culminating in real music and real painting.

The three scenes of *Ghost Sonata* are best thought of as three movements: the first largely expository, introducing and interweaving the play's many themes; the second, intensely dramatic; and the third, predominantly lyrical. The two main characters are an old man and a young man, Hummel and the Student, who meet in scene i; Hummel is again central in scene ii, and the Student – in what is virtually a duet with the Young Lady – in scene iii. There are many subsidiary figures, all distinct and significant, with their own stories, many of which are related in anecdote by Hummel to the Student in the first scene. All are symbolic, and it is not difficult to identify a dominant quality in each: innocence, vanity, tyranny, remorse and many more. Yet more than one such quality is associated with most of the figures; they are not simply allegorical, to be mechanically interpreted in a single, indisputable way. A valid analogy can be drawn between them and musical motifs, or, perhaps, instruments in a small orchestra, some of which are featured in solo passages, all being sharply distinguishable at particular moments. In the second scene, Hummel continues to be the chief soloist, as in scene i, but the Mummy challenges his dominance in the middle of the scene, and the Student's voice, actually singing to harp accompaniment, closes the scene. The same song is repeated at the end of the third scene and, although Hummel has passed out of the play at the end of scene ii, a reminder of him – the Hummel theme – intrudes into the young couple's love duet in the person of the grotesque Cook 'of the Hummel family of vampires'. The gnomic lines of the Student's song (drawn from the thirteenth-century Icelandic 'Lay of the Sun') are an explicit, verbal summing-up of the main themes on which Strindberg has constructed *Ghost Sonata*:

> I saw the sun. To me it seemed
> that I beheld the Hidden.
> Men must reap what they have sown,
> blest is he whose deeds are good.
> Deeds which you have wrought in fury,
> cannot in evil find redress.
> Comfort him you have distressed
> with loving-kindness – this will heal.
> No fear has he who does no ill.
> Sweet is innocence.
>
> (trans. Elizabeth Sprigge, *Six Plays*, p. 295)

Nothing else in *Ghost Sonata* is didactic in this way, though good and evil are certainly in conflict in various forms in the play.

In the first two scenes the dramatic development takes us from values associated with the Old Testament to those of the New or, to change the terms, from a condition in which the image of an all-powerful father prevails to the checking of this power and turning away of vengeance by mercy through the person of the benevolent mother. We seem to be in the world of folk tale when Director Hummel, in his wheel chair, tells the brave young Student about the house before them and its inhabitants and promises to send him on an adventure which will make his fortune and lead to marriage with the beautiful Young Lady. Hummel's view of human beings and their destinies is scorchingly satirical, and his arrogance takes emblematic form when the beggars draw him along, a crippled tyrant in his triumphal chariot. His horror at the apparition of the milkmaid in the attitude of a drowning girl is a forceful sign of the guiltiness of the self-appointed judge (a moment repeated in scene ii as part of the pattern).

Particularly characteristic of *Ghost Sonata* is the presentation of ideas in concrete form as dynamic stage images. The woman who has shrivelled into age, going through the motions and speaking the commonplaces of a stagnant life, is imaged as a Mummy, living in a cupboard and talking like a parrot. The contrast with her lost youth is ever-present in the marble statue of a beautiful girl, an image of the eternal feminine which links past and present, the Mummy's youth and her daughter's present loveliness, and appears, when the blind is drawn up, as a visual counterpoint to the immobile figure of the woman in black on the stairs, at the start of the scene, as it does to the Milkmaid, frozen in her gesture of despair, at the end. The ghost supper itself, which occupies scene ii, is a similar metaphysical image: a ritual gathering of old acquaintances who know each other so well that they have nothing to say, it is also a mutual haunting as they all munch in silence over the guilty secrets which hold them together. The grotesque quality of the gathering is summed up in the moment when Hummel, who has come to strip away the veil – to purify or simply punish, bangs on the table with his crutch. But the Mummy, his former lover, after years of remorse has another kind of power to check him – emblematically again, – by stopping the clock before it can strike twelve. The cupboard from which she came, and into which he now goes, apparently to hang himself, is another box, like the telephone kiosk, a container for a puppet or such an *Übermarionette* as Gordon Craig, prophet and pioneer of a modern visionary theatre, wanted as replacement for the egotistical self-projection of contemporary actors. In the first, exterior scene, indeed, the various windows of the house may suggest and even function as so many such booths, or little proscenium openings.

The disposal of Hummel dislocates the plot, but also clears the way for the scene in the hyacinth room, which at first, like Fingal's Cave in *A Dream Play*, seems to be a meeting-place of earth and heaven. (The key images and concepts are again Buddhist.) However, the mood of young love and hope shifts jarringly into another key: as in the relationship between the Daughter and the Lawyer in the earlier play, so now the experience of domesticity, and return to all the petty irritations of everyday life in an epitome of marriage, distort love to ugliness. The new mood is presided over by the comic, vulgar and abrasive, stubbornly real, yet swollen and surreal figure of the Cook, irrepressible reminder of the materiality of life and all the tyrannies of social relationships and mutual dependencies in particular. The end of the dramatic action, with the wilting and dying of the Young Lady, has been variously interpreted. Certainly it is the end of a dream in more than one sense, leaving the Student sadder and wiser at the end of his adventure. (One Ingmar Bergman production[4] and some subsequent interpretations suggest that the Student has seduced and virtually murdered his love, as Hummel did the Milkmaid long ago.) The dying process is as unrealistic as most other incidents in the play, and it seems to have been ordained all along, an early pointer being the slipping of her bracelet from the Young Lady's over-thin wrist and hand. The drawing of the oriental screen around her at the final moment is an alternative way of putting a marionette in a box, when it is no longer needed in the performance, and it emphasises how tenuous the existence of the ideal girl always was.

Strindberg directed that when the harp sounds again and the Student's song is heard a second time, the stage picture should give way to a back projection of Böcklin's picture, 'The Isle of the Dead'. If the instruction is followed, it ensures some moments of contemplation, a stasis, between the ending of the dramatic action and the release of audience attention, moments before people can shift in their seats and the applause begin. This balances the start of the play; but now the picture imposes, or confirms, a very different mood, with its eeerie, chilling, remote beauty. Even the moralism of the song is absorbed into this evocation of the peace of death.

T. S. Eliot wrote his own *Ghost Sonata* in *The Family Reunion*, and there are numerous lines in that play which reflect not only on *Ghost Sonata* but on several of the other works Strindberg wrote for the stage from *Crimes and Crimes* onward:

> . . . the things that are going to happen
> Have already happened;

Perhaps my life has only been a dream
Dreamt through me by the minds of others;

What we have written is not a story of detection,
Of crime and punishment, but of sin and expiation;

and life has to be lived, decisions taken, 'in the ring of ghosts'.

10
Strindberg and the Theatre

Britain and America

In 1949, Michael Redgrave, then playing in Strindberg's *The Father*, made a ceremonial river journey to Gravesend, bearing a commemorative plaque. It was the centenary of August Strindberg's birth, and the plaque acknowledged that Sweden's great dramatist had arrived in London via a sea-crossing to Gravesend, in 1893, with his second wife, the Austrian Frida Uhl. Financially desperate, they had come over in response to signs of interest in his works, with over-sanguine hopes that England could become the scene of a Strindberg theatre.[1]

During the 1890s, Strindberg's name was invoked by the champions of Ibsen who wanted a censorship-free theatre. Translations of his novels and tales and extracts from his notebooks found publishers then and up to the First World War, while a few of his plays achieved an occasional theatre-club performance.[2] He was identified with Naturalism on account of his Preface to *Miss Julie*, knowledge of which came to England through André Antoine's Théâtre Libre presentation in Paris, in 1893. It is understandable that a rather lop-sided view of his achievement should have reached English-speaking readers. The *persona* of the novels was readily identified with the author, and the legend of a gloomy Swedish madman obscured the qualities of robust humour, shrewdness, tenderness and lyrical beauty to be found in his work, alongside its savage energy.

Though N. Erichsen's translation of *The Father* into English was published in 1899, long before any of Strindberg's other plays, the first London performance of the work was in Yiddish, when Maurice Moscovitch, an actor from Odessa who became famous in America and England, played it at the Pavilion Theatre, Whitechapel, in 1910/11. Technically private performances of both *The Father* and *Miss Julie* were given in English by a group called the Adelphi Play Society in 1911 and 1912 respectively, a translation of the second being provided by Bernard Shaw's sister, Lucy. Silent-screen star Nazimova, in *Miss Julie*, introduced Strindberg to New York in 1905. In 1912, the year of the dramatist's death, his great historical drama, *Gustav Vasa*, directed by Per Lindberg, was performed in Swedish in Chicago, and *Easter* was presented in the same city in 1913. A larger body of Strindberg's plays now became available through American translations: a collection by Edith and Warner Öland, which included a number of minor pieces, and the multi-volume authorised translations of Edwin Björkman. Warner Öland, a Hollywood star, played the lead in *The Father* at the Berkeley Theatre, New York in 1912. In the next decade, a British devotee of the drama, Pax Robertson, took advantage of Björkman's translations to include a whole series of Strindberg plays in the programmes of world theatre shown to London audiences at the Chelsea Art Theatre, in Upper Manor Street: *Easter*, *The Outlaw* (an early one-act play), *Swanwhite* and *Thunderstorm*, all first presented in 1922; *After the Fire* (attended by Sweden's Crown Prince, with the Ambassador, Baron Palmstierna) and *Debit and Credit* in 1923; *Simoon* in 1924; *Pariah* in 1925; *Advent* in 1929; and *A Dream Play* in 1930. Pax Robertson played all the female leads herself and regarded public performance as incidental to work on the plays, rather than as her main goal.

Robert Atkins prepared a production of *Advent* for the Royal Victoria Hall (Old Vic) in 1921. As he was taken ill, the work was completed by Hubert Hine. In the following year, *The Father* was first licensed by the Lord Chamberlain for a production at the Apollo Theatre under J. B. Fagan's management, which was not, in fact, given. Fagan moved to the Oxford Playhouse where he presented *The Stronger* in 1924, *Creditors*, directed by Allan Wade, in 1925, and *The Spook Sonata* (with Elliott Seabrooke as Hummel, Veronica Turleigh and Glen Byam Shaw) in 1926. A matinée of the same production was given at the Globe Theatre, London, in May of that year (with Allan Jeayes replacing Elliott Seabrooke and Mary Grey in place of Veronica Turleigh). Sir St. Vincent Troubridge recalled being front-of-house manager when this was transferred to the Strand Theatre for one week in June, 1927, and mentioned his surprise that the production 'grossed £500 on the week, which though much below expenses, was remarkable for such a play at that time in the West End'.[3] After being revived at the Oxford Playhouse in 1928, *The Spook Sonata* was transferred to the Cambridge Festival Theatre. Fagan's success with this play counts as the decisive factor in making *Ghost Sonata* (to give it the title now preferred) one of Strindberg's best-known plays in England today, alongside *The Father*, *Miss Julie* and *The Dance of Death* (which, probably through a general shift in public taste, has taken over this position from *Easter*). Fagan's last Strindberg production at Oxford was of *Crimes and Crimes*, under the title of *Intoxication* (from the German *Rausch*, the name of Ernst Lubitsch's film version – with Astá Nielsen as Henriette – made in 1919, before his departure for Hollywood).

There had been American performances of *Creditors* (in Boston and Chicago) and *The Road to Damascus* (New York, 1914–15) before the 1920's when the Provincetown Players were encouraged by Eugene O'Neill to present *Ghost Sonata* (1924) and *A Dream Play* (1926): an adventurous choice, corresponding to, and always acknowledging, the debt O'Neill's own drama owes to Strindberg. The influence of *Miss Julie* and *A Dream Play* on Bernard Shaw's *Arms and the Man* and *Heartbreak House* respectively is more open to speculation. However, when Shaw received the Nobel Prize for Literature in 1926, he gave the money to subsidise the publication of Swedish plays in English translations. As a result, the Anglo-Swedish Literary Foundation published, volume by volume until the Second World War, a medley of versions by different hands in what was nevertheless the first strictly English collection of Strindberg's drama.

In 1927, the direction of the Everyman Theatre, Hampstead, was in the hands of Malcolm Morley and Milton Rosmer. Morley had spent some time acting in America and struck up a friendship with Eugene O'Neill. During a summer in New London, Connecticut, the two had read voraciously in European philosophy and modern literature, and Morley had come to share O'Neill's excitement over Strindberg. His spell with Rosmer at the Everyman was coming to an end, and the money was running out; with nothing to lose, as it seemed, they could have their last fling with an impossible play: *The Father*. Peter Godfrey had produced *The Dance of Death* at his Gate Theatre Club in Covent Garden in 1925; and the Morley–Rosmer production might have created as slight a ripple in theatrical history if it had not been for the actor who was eventually persuaded to play Adolf, the Captain. Robert Loraine had been a star from the beginning of the century up to the First World War: an actor of immense verve who could carry off heroic roles, he also excelled in certain kinds of comedy. His greatest successes were Cyrano de Bergerac, and Tanner in Shaw's *Man and Superman*. He had taken to the war with zest, had become an air ace with the Royal Flying Corps, been decorated and so badly wounded that a less determined man might well have had no further civilian career. Yet he had struggled back to the stage in his old parts. After his initial hesitation about this new role, he entered with great seriousness on the preparatory study. His wife later described how he visited London asylums to observe the insane and incorporated into his acting a few selected gestures:

> The first was an upward forked movement of the right hand; in the second, he went down alternately on his right or left knee, whichever one gave under him with the blackness of despair; it was a movement in which he fell and rose, as some kind of spiritual fight went on. And the third . . . conveyed a 'blotting out'. Yet it was merely standing with the top of the forehead pressed against a wall or door.[4]

A comment from the actor himself is concerned more with internal acting and control:

> The secret of playing the Father does not lie in letting yourself go, but in having enough power to suppress. The acts of violence . . . spin downwards, uncontrolled, involuntarily out of the burden of his mind. They are not built up effects as far as the expression of force and vigour goes, but spasms from the pent-up suffering within him. Noise is always empty. Force is conveyed by what you suppress.[5]

Surviving photographs convey the intensity of pain and the uncomfortable authenticity Loraine brought to his portrayal of a man whose sense of reality dissolves through his wife's deliberate manipulation of facts and incidents. (Dorothy Dix was a formidable and stony Laura.)

As so often in the theatre, it was undoubtedly the quality of mesmeric acting that turned the Everyman production into a sensation and caused its prompt transfer to the Savoy Theatre on 23 August 1927. Yet Milton Rosmer's contribution, in directing and designing the play, matched Loraine's imaginatively. The set had unexpected features: an immense window, suggesting icy bleakness beyond, unnervingly contrasted with tall pampas grass in a brass pot; an oak door beside it, which opened on a snowy yard; and a turret staircase. None of these appeared in Strindberg's description of the set he had in mind, though there were hints here of the fortified isolation he gave to another fraught marriage, in *The Dance of Death*. The solidity of the oak furnishings was belied by lighting effects that may have been suggested by the practice of Strindberg's own Intimate Theatre in Stockholm between 1906 and 1911. The set had blue-green walls, and amber spots played on it, creating amorphous, shifting, purple shadows, 'so that the walls, although definite, became atmospheric and symbolic. And the room, which was not so much a room as an enclosure, either widened or contracted with the mood.'[5] Actors and directors are more powerful interpreters of drama than scholars and critics can ever be; and it was not Strindberg the champion of naturalism, identified with the Preface to *Miss Julie*, who was made known to the London public in 1927. Following *Ghost Sonata*, it was the symbolic sub-structure of *The Father* and the way it can drag at the spectator's secret fears that this production revealed. The Everyman production was revived at the Apollo Theatre, with the same principals, in 1929. In the intervening year, Loraine appeared as Edgar in *The Dance of Death* at the same theatre. Also in the wake of the Rosmer–Loraine triumph came a production of *Easter*, in 1928, at the Arts Theatre Club, with Gwen Frangçon Davies in the lead as Eleanora, and Peggy Ashcroft as Christina.

When the critic for *The World* saw Maurice Elvey's production of *Miss Julie* in 1912, he registered it as 'the most brutal and repellant play we have ever had to sit through'. Desmond MacCarthy, having watched an obscure production with Hilda Maude as Miss Julie, in 1927, described his response, in retrospect, as 'depressed equanimity': 'Well, well, she cut her throat and her father rang for his boots and breakfast'. It had taken the Pitoëffs' company visiting the Arts Theatre Club from the Paris Théâtre de l'Avénue in February 1933 – and playing in French – to bring him a very different experience. His review in *The New Statesman and Nation* concentrated on Ludmilla Pitoëff's performance, summed up as 'subtle and thorough, violent and delicate, moving and strange'. What is of more general significance is that Mme. Pitoëff's interpretation of Julie as a wilful child who brings disaster down on herself, without realising the monstrous consequences that will follow from the amusement she so easily and arrogantly indulges in, made the play 'more interesting and far more moving' than if the heroine appears as the neurotic, hysterical young woman identified in Strindberg's Preface: 'it makes the close tragic instead of pathological'. The detailed emotional naturalism of the acting – 'We watch a hard little face quivering, now and then, with the excitement of playing with fire'; 'I have never seen on the stage a more complete representation in gait, gesture, expression, of the complete paralysis of the will by terror and regret' – led MacCarthy to recognise that Strindberg's drama did not have to be interpreted for its curiosity value, and that knowledge of the author's life had been used to limit and chain his work in the past: 'as handled by the Pitoëffs all that disappeared from the play'.

The ban on public performances of *Miss Julie* in England was first lifted in 1939, since when it has become a favourite in the repertoire. It has the practical advantage of not costing too much to mount and having only three speaking parts. Yet it also offers one of the very finest roles written for a woman (along with its lineal descendant, Tennessee Williams' *Streetcar Named Desire*), and Sonia Dresdel, Diane Cilento, Jill Bennett, Maggie Smith and, most recently, Cheryl Campbell have been among the leading actresses to tackle it. In 1949, the centenary year, a thoughtful production by Peter Cotes, with an electric performance by Joan Miller, transferred from Manchester's Library Theatre to the Lyric, Hammersmith.

Caspar Wrede, arranging his audience on three sides of a rectangular playing area, at the Edinburgh Festival fringe of 1953, and Stephen Joseph's Theatre-in-the-Round company, in 1960, tested new ways of achieving the intimacy and tension Strindberg wanted in the mutual seduction, and destruction, of the lady and the servant.

Appropriately, *Miss Julie* has found its way to the small screen: an Independent Television broadcast in 1956 matched Mai Zetterling's Julie with Tyrone Power's Jean; but more satisfying was the television film based on Robin Phillips's RSC production at The Place (with Helen Mirren as Julie), which developed the interlude – the duration of the sex act, when the peasants invade the stage – into a grave and eerie ritual. A freer treatment, following a straight presentation of the play, was Steven Berkoff's deconstruction, entitled *Miss Julie versus Expressionism* (ICA, 1973), which isolated and repeated the images of (ringmaster's) whip and top hat, the boots, chopper and razor, the fishnet-clad ankle and the feathers of the destroyed bird (key images from the original play) to bring out the sado-masochistic pattern in the sexual politics Strindberg's text reveals.

The National Theatre twice contributed to bringing Strindberg to wider public attention before the Company left the Old Vic for its new premises: by staging in London Michael Elliott's 1966 Chichester Festival production of *Miss Julie* with Maggie Smith and Albert Finney; and, in 1967, by presenting an abridgment and conflation of the two parts of *The Dance of Death*. The robust glee Laurence Olivier brought to the playing of Edgar was authentically Strindbergian. A cartoon by Gerald Scarfe caught better than the photographs the splendid viciousness with which he and Alice (Geraldine McEwan) celebrated the hellish security of their marriage. This production hardly negotiated the ambivalence of the play as a whole: the world that, as Strindberg imagines it, only *seems* real was too realistic, and the effectiveness of the play depended wholly on the acting. Still, it did succeed in conveying that *The Dance of Death* is a kind of savage comedy, and it encouraged further attempts on the play in other parts of

Britain. It was seen in Leicester in 1982 and at the Manchester Royal Exchange in 1983.

Although *The Father* has been tackled less often, the work of British directors has certainly made this work part of the classic repertoire of our theatre. Peter Cotes's direction of this play for an Arts Theatre season in 1953 certainly counts among the few great Strindberg occasions in Britain. As a spin-off from it, Cotes directed *The Father* in Elizabeth Sprigge's translation as the first-ever Independent Television drama production, contracted to fill a one-hour slot, on 27 June 1957. Robert Shaw later played Adolf on BBC television (21 September 1962), marking fifty years since the dramatist's death. Since 1957, there are many people who rarely go to the theatre, and never read drama, who recall this play; and some even add that, terrifying as it was, it stirred an element of recognition – that marriage can be like that!

Wilfred Lawson had played the Captain at the Arts Theatre: 'the only *great* actor I have ever seen', said Grace Wyndham Goldie.[6] 'I was simply bowled over by this fantastic, fabulous genius', reported Joseph Losey, who went back five or six times to watch the performance and had Donald Ogden Stewart prepare a screenplay of *The Father*. The plan to film it came to nothing in the end, as Lawson and conventional contractual arrangements could not be made to fit. Like Robert Loraine, Lawson had been badly wounded in the First World War, and in addition he was an epileptic and heavy drinker. (He appears, leaning against the car, in the well-known photograph of George Devine's brave young English Stage Company, taken in front of the Royal Court Theatre in 1956.) He simulated an epileptic fit nightly in the course of the play, an electrifying incident in a performance on the heroic scale, yet rooted in human compassion. A big man, he seemed far larger than life-size in intellect and stage presence. Beatrix Lehmann, who brought her usual power of controlled tragic intensity to the part of Laura, commented on the qualities of another age in Lawson's playing, especially his distinctive, fathomless voice: 'Wilfred had this declaiming voice and the onomatopoeics used in the time of Irving'. It suited the gathering rhythms and poetic quality, gradually built up as the play goes on.

Cotes used the small stage of the Arts Theatre to claustrophobic effect, turning it into a stuffy nineteenth-century parlour, comfortably furnished, walls lined with dark silk and curtained to match, the lamp resting on a heavily draped table. His set showed a tree outside the window, and a grandfather clock measured the action with a loud insistent tick. Strong lighting on the faces and a trick of leaving the perimeter of the set in shadow allowed emotional reality to gain an ascendancy over mere realism and gave the more mysterious qualities in the play their chance. The fearfulness of the young girl at her grandmother's spiritualistic practices, and running scared from a strange song in the attic, was credible in itself and contributed to the atmosphere of gathering unseen presences, as the old Nurse, reading her hymnbook in the pool of light cast on the table, murmured the words of the *Dies Irae*.

In the first scene, Lawson established the robust commonsense normality of the Captain, the easily assertive manner of a mature man accustomed to be obeyed, his brusqueness hinting at contempt for his parson brother-in-law, as later for the doctor, his sardonic humour a strength which let him shrug off the irritations and disappointments of life. Flinging out of the house of women into the storm was the action of one unafraid of those elemental forces; but, in the house, he was caught and caged. He recalled (as Strindberg certainly intended) Shakespeare's use of the storm in *King Lear*: raging without, joined and matched by an equal elemental fury in the tragic hero's mind. A dark surround dissolved the walls of the room as Lawson broke onto the stage through the papered-over door, a man seeking a way through the shadows in his mind: a terrifying figure now, not because of his craziness, but because the human being had acquired titanic stature. This was grandeur, capable of a monumental calm and reasonableness, punctuated by outbursts of truth from the abyss and explosions of destructive energy and pain, revealing not individual neurosis but the bedrock of the first scene's commonplaces, contemplated and felt without remission.[6]

Beatrix Lehmann created a Laura of ambiguous quality, a woman and not a monster of treachery and malice. The performance rested squarely on Laura's claim that her actions were dictated by something greater than her personal will. This was an unsmiling, disenchanted wife with an arrogance of her own, resentful and opportunistic, determined to fight for her child and her personal status, yet capable of relaxing into an intimacy of shared memories and even mutual understanding with the one closest to her in the world. Lawson lay on the couch and she leant against it, sitting close beside him on the floor, in that lull while the two characters contemplate the distant days of their courtship, when hope was still alive, that is the immediate prelude to his throwing of the lamp at her. Thus a link was made between the bed of love and the cradle-bier which the couch becomes at the end of the play, confining the man as surely as the straitjacket which renews the swaddling bands on the newly born – and which drew Laura's appalled yet fascinated gaze.

Vivien Merchant, in Keith Hack's production at Greenwich, more than twenty years later, made Laura the more obviously neurotic of the couple: a woman whose situation has perverted her into nagging, whining vengefulness. Although psychologically persuasive in itself, this portrayal made it more difficult to accept the extent to which she carries the doctor, and eventually the parson and the Captain's batman, Nöjd, along with her. The struggle of the child caught in this malign situation came over more strongly than usual.

Charles Marowitz's free adaptation of *The Father*, the final production of his Open Space theatre, late in 1979, simplified the play into a violent ritual of militant feminism. It was a fitting sequel to the 'Theatre of Cruelty' productions he had worked on with Peter Brook in the previous decade. Although Marowitz has described the original play as 'a private hallucination disguised as a naturalistic drama',[7] implying that it is an expression of Strindberg's personal fear of women, his own version had a quality of mythic universality: the projection of a general male nightmare of female power. As in his Shakespeare collages, so here Marowitz gave the performance a heightened rhythm of repeated precipitate movement suddenly arrested, and a technique of lighting which snapped from realistic clarity to catch dramatic images or tableaux in a lurid glare and then plunged into blackout. Strindberg's allusions to Greek myth were reflected in the set: floorboards slanted in exaggerated perspective (reminiscent of a Munch picture) towards a massive door, evoking some ancient palace or temple. (Denholm Elliott's Captain was first seen framed on its threshold.) Yet these seemingly permanent features were transformed or dissolved as if under the pressure of mental agitation. The action alternated between snatches of domestic realism and hallucinatory sequences, with the various women characters, led by Diane Cilento as Laura, with Veronica Quilligan as an eroticised Bertha, shifting out of their distinct identities to form a composite, impersonal image of female nature. The lamp-throwing episode was especially memorable: one side of the stage seemed to explode in flames, with a crack of thunder, as wife, nurse and daughter, moving as one, advanced on the Captain out of the darkness, thrusting their flaming torches into his face. Powerful as the symbolic action was, in this version, the moving human quality retained in the Cotes–Lawson production was inevitably lost.

When Ingmar Bergman's production of *A Dream Play* visited the Aldwych Theatre in 1971, it made no great impact. There was as yet no British tradition of stage interpretation for it to engage with,[8] but, following a staging of the play in Belfast, in 1973, the Traverse Theatre, Edinburgh, in 1974 presented Bergman's adaptation in the round, using a set of ladders and split levels perhaps suggested by photographs surviving from Artaud's 1928 production. The role of Agnes (the Daughter) was split between three actresses (Bergman had made Agnes and Indra's Daughter two separate characters) suggesting a possibly distracting allusion to the dramatist's three wives. Roger Kemp played the Poet, in whose consciousness Bergman located the play, and James Snell the Officer, while the other actors each combined three or four roles (Roy Marsden appearing as the Lawyer and Simon Callow as the Quarantine Master, but each playing minor roles besides). The audience was deeply impressed, finding the play intense, painful and beautiful. Mike Ockrent, the director, together with David Gothard, went on to tackle a version of all three parts of *To Damascus* at the same theatre in 1975. 'There wasn't a weak link in the performance', reported Cordelia Oliver, in *The Guardian*. She also equated the Stranger simply with Strindberg, though Roy Marsden filled the role in Part I and Ron Forfar in

Parts II and III (presented together on alternate nights, except on one occasion when the three sections were played in the one evening). The theatre lived up to its name by using a narrow platform, running through the auditorium from end to end. A succession of symbolic objects or properties marked the scenic stations in the hero's dramatic pilgrimage. The general style of the production came close to the fantastic realism established by the chief of Swedish interpreters of Strindberg's drama, Olof Molander, over a thirty-year period. Emotional truth in the acting was the keynote of this approach.

Although forms of dramatic expression have been acceptable in the British theatre since the 1950's which earlier would have met with blank hostility, and Harold Pinter, especially, has expressed certain truths about the individual's encounter with the world that are embedded in Strindberg's dramatic practice, this more recent period has been marked by increasing imaginative attention to a few Strindberg plays rather than exploration of the wider range of his work.[9] The main national companies have been particularly timid. Over the years, listeners to BBC Radio have been able to hear many of the plays. (The exceptions have been the whole range of history plays, some of the early plays, including *Sir Bengt's Wife*, a few short pieces and the last of the chamber plays, *The Black Glove*.) In addition, there have been two fine television broadcasts of *Ghost Sonata*: the first directed by Stuart Burge in 1962, with Robert Helpmann as Hummel and Beatrix Lehmann as the Mummy, and Philip Saville's production in 1980, with Donald Pleasence and Lila Kedrova. This last used a translation by Michael Meyer, whose versions of Strindberg's plays have been a valuable resource for British performances over the last twenty years, though they cover a far smaller part of his total dramatic work than the

American versions of Arvid Paulson, Evert Sprinchorn and Walter Johnson.

The Strindberg centenary was marked in New York by a production of *The Father* at the 49th Street Theatre, with Raymond Massey as the Captain, Grace Kelly playing the daughter. Except for this, Elisabeth Bergner's tour in *Miss Julie*, 1947, and Viveca Lindfors' appearance in the same play at the Phoenix, New York, in 1956, most of the Strindberg plays seen in the United States between the 1920's and 1970's were college theatre productions. In 1970, Rip Torn and Viveca Lindfors were seen in *Dance of Death* at the Arena Theatre, Washington, moving to New York in 1971. Rip Torn appeared again in New York in a 1976 season of *Creditors, Miss Julie* and *The Stronger* with Geraldine Page.

Europe

The Father and *Miss Julie*, have, indeed, been performed all over the world from South America to Japan. Historically interesting performances of other Strindberg plays and also the work of directors who have dedicated years to the exploration of his drama have more particular interest here. Immediately before the outbreak of the First World War, Strindberg was the most produced of modern dramatists in Germany. (This was made possible through the availability of his collected plays in a German translation.) Although he became the most closely identified with a new style of staging Strindberg, Max Reinhardt was in fact one director among many in Germany who turned some attention to his plays between the early years of the century and the end of the 1920s. Reinhardt began in 1902–04 with intimate theatre productions of the naturalistic pieces: *The Stronger*, *The Bond* and *Miss Julie* and the transitional

Rausch (*Crimes and Crimes*). However, Reinhardt's main achievement was a series of productions which took off from the style, based on distortion, which he first tried for Ibsen's *Ghosts* in 1906, using designs commissioned from Edvard Munch. The tally of further Reinhardt productions of Strindberg is as follows: *The Dance of Death* (1912); *Storm* (1913); *The Pelican* (1914); *The Father* (1915); *Ghost Sonata* and *Master Olof* (1916); *The Black Glove* (1918); *Advent* (1919); *The Burned House* (1920); *A Dream Play* (as guest director at Dramaten, 1921; then in Berlin with a German company). These productions made considerable use of silence as part of the overall rhythm and employed music skilfully to increase the eerie, dreamlike quality in the plays, while retaining an element of realism. In the chamber plays and *A Dream Play*, Reinhardt developed a technique of spotlighting figures, or heads, against dark backgrounds, using a gauze to make unlit areas seem invisible in *Ghost Sonata*. The critic Siegfried Jacobsohn commented, 'Reinhardt's ear hears all of Strindberg's music, even its dissonances, without attempting to make harmonies of them. He venerates the Strindberg who is kind beyond measure, just as he does the one who is tortured beyond measure. . . . He carries the victims of this fanatic lover of truth into an atmosphere so distorted, so gloomy, so full of fantastic life and motion, that it might be Van Gogh's.'[10]

The première of *A Dream Play* in Berlin had taken place in 1916, under Rudolf Bernauer's direction, with sets designed by the Dane, Svend Gade, which accentuated the spiritual, dreamlike quality and were influential for a long time. (Svend Gade had already been responsible for designing *The Crown Bride* for the same theatre in 1913 and was to direct and design a production of *Sir Bengt's Wife* in Berlin in 1920, after mounting *A Dream Play* in

1917, and *Advent* in 1918 at the Dagmar Theatre, Copenhagen.) But no German presentation of a Strindberg play had greater impact than *Charles XII*, directed by Gustav Hartung at Darmstadt in 1924, then seen at the Lessing Theatre in Berlin, the following year. Judged by some to be a distortion of Strindberg's play, it went to the limits of expressionism to create the sense of apocalypse. Oscar Homolka's playing of the Man was much praised.

After the Second World War, Oscar Fritz Schuh presided over a Strindberg revival at the Theater am Kurfürstendamm in West Berlin, which included another production of *Charles XII* in 1956. This suggested a parallel between Sweden's warrior-king and Hitler and between Charles's death and Hitler's end in the bunker. Schuh's production of *A Dream Play* (1955) was seen in London at Sadlers Wells. Characters approached and receded slowly, on a conveyor belt. Strindberg's original suggestions had some influence on the staging, particularly in the marking of scenic locations by symbolic objects, which in this case were lowered from the flies, and the use of wings (or periaktoi) bearing non-naturalistic designs. Salvador Dali's influence on the visual style was cited, but was not evident in the consistently sombre colours, black and white, grey and brown.

Meyerhold is recorded as having produced Strindberg's naturalistic plays in the early years of this century (*The Father*, 1904/5; *Miss Julie*, 1906). Rather more information is available about his production of *Crimes and Crimes* in 1912, the year of Strindberg's death. He made systematic use of colour symbolism (increasingly important in Strindberg's later plays) and kept his actors still, except when movement was intended to carry strong significance. He set the scene by means of a painted backcloth deeply recessed within a broad black frame, so that the main stage interest was concentrated strongly on the actors. However, the most famous Russian production of Strindberg was directed by Evgeni Vahtangov, whose ambition was to combine all he had learned from Meyerhold about non-naturalistic staging and acrobatically-based playing with the emotional and psychological depth of performance cultivated by Stanislavski. *Erik XIV* (in the First Studio of the Moscow Art Theatre) was one of the three great productions of Vahtangov's *annus mirabilis*, 1921, the year before his premature death. He used sets and costumes to develop the relevance of the play to the Bolshevik revolution and as a protest against any possibility of a single man holding the reins of power over a people. He accentuated a contrast between two worlds in the play: one vital (seen in the common people and especially in Karin, Erik's commoner-queen, and her burgher father) and the other moribund (the world of the nobles at court), made evident in a grotesque style of playing, as well as make-up, costumes and court settings. The production, with music by Rachmaninov, was taken to Berlin in 1922. Michael Chekhov, the great writer's nephew, played Erik there as in Moscow; and he repeated his performance when he led the company presenting the same play in Paris in 1931, as guests at Dullin's Théâtre de l'Atelier.[11]

Strindberg's work went virtually unperformed in France between the Théâtre Libre and Théâtre de l'Oeuvre performances in the 1890s and a revival of interest in the 1920s. Anthony Swerling has thoroughly documented his influence on French writers and the French theatre thereafter up to 1960. For our present purpose, the plays directed by Jean Vilar form the most striking group in their variety: *The Dance of Death* and *Storm* in 1943 and *Erik XIV* in 1960, the last being the most lavishly spectacular, the first probably more dramatically effective (Vilar played the leads himself). The most visionary approach to Strindberg's work in France had undoubtedly been the single production of *A Dream Play* by Antonin Artaud's Théâtre Alfred Jarry in 1928, taken together with Artaud's project for mounting *Ghost Sonata* in 1931, unrealised as that was. His break of two years previously with the Surrealists led to an organised disturbance which distracted attention from the play itself, yet many members of the distinguished audience were interested and moved by it; some liked it better than Reinhardt's version. Artaud's general aim was to use theatre for the release of humanity's inner life, and he saw Strindberg's post-Inferno drama as perfectly suited to his purpose. Seeking freedom of expression from all theatrical conventions, he entirely abandoned pictorial setting in favour of the simplicity of functional screens and ladders which aided the reality of three-dimensional performance in space. Where he pioneered, Roger Blin's 1949 presentation of *Ghost Sonata* at the Gaieté, Montparnasse, and Raymond Rouleau's of *A Dream Play* at the Comédie-Française in 1970, were ultimately to follow.

Probably the most interesting Strindberg production in western Europe in recent years has been the staging of *Storm* by Giorgio Strehler's company of the Piccolo Theatre of Milan in 1980, subsequently toured. Strehler interposed a wall of black glass between the audience and the house and introduced various anti-realistic touches (including a piano which – like the harp in *Ghost Sonata* – played without human agency), employing background music full of dissonances, and exploiting Strindberg's signals for lightning flashes to juxtapose brilliant visual clarity with total darkness. It is a good example of how modern directors have taken their cue from *Ghost Sonata* for the production of the other chamber plays.

The history of Strindberg production in Sweden has, of

course, particular authority, but also some diversity. The work of August Falck in co-operation with Strindberg has already been considered. Other contemporary directors whose approach to his plays Strindberg was able to judge were Albert Ranft and Harald Molander, Emil Grandinson and Victor Castegren. He was happiest with Grandinson's presentation of *To Damascus* which extended the stage with steps and made it possible for certain scenes to be recessed behind a semi-circular arch which created a form of inner stage. The Ranft and Molander productions at Dramaten were marked by a realistic solidity and literalness; Castegren's staging of *A Dream Play* disappointed, by contrast, in that the inadequate use of machinery turned the attempt at imaginative freedom into earthbound devices, a 'materialisation phenomenon'.

Knut Ström who, as a young man, had worked as a designer for Intiman, went on to direct at Düsseldorf Schauspielhaus, where he presented *Crimes and Crimes* (1916), *Storm* and *The Pelican* in 1917 and *A Dream Play* in 1918. His designs for the last have a patterned elegance, a two-dimensional flatness of effect, calculated to banish emotional vagueness or sentimentality. Ström then joined Per Lindberg, director of the new and well-equipped Lorensberg Theatre in Göteborg, who had studied the work of Reinhardt and the ideas of Meyerhold. Together they inaugurated theatrical modernism in Sweden, collaborating first on *Gustav Vasa* (1919) and *Creditors* (1920). Later in 1920, Lindberg directed the verse *Master Olof* and *The Saga of the Folkungs* triumphantly, both with striking designs by Ström. (Their repertoire was generally classic, not limited to Strindberg's plays.) Ström himself directed, as well as designing, *Crimes and Crimes* in 1921, the world première of *To Damascus* III in 1922, the lyric drama, *The Flying Dutchman*, the following year, and *To*

Damascus II at the same theatre in 1924.[12] Ström also directed Strindberg's *Gustav Adolf* at the Lorensberg Theatre in 1932. That theatre was replaced by the fine Göteborg City Theatre (which he designed) in 1934, and Ström mounted further Strindberg plays there in later years, most notably *Crimes and Crimes* with Karin Kavli as Henriette and Maria Schildknecht, who had belonged to the Falck–Strindberg company, as Mme. Cathérine, for the Strindberg centenary in 1949. He produced *Advent* and *Storm* in 1951 and *Gustav Vasa* as late as 1955, at the same theatre.

The most devoted and influential Swedish director of Strindbergian drama was Olof Molander, chief of Dramaten, 1934–38, when some of his finest work was done, though the list of his Strindberg productions in various parts of Scandinavia extends from the 1920s to the 1960s. Apart from radio presentations, there is a notable absence of the frequently seen naturalistic plays from this list. The subjective aspect was Molander's special concern, and the moving, human content of his work was constantly praised. Certainly he reaped the benefit of a knowledge of Strindberg's text unrivalled in depth and intimacy. He explored *A Dream Play* in seven distinct productions, *Ghost Sonata* in four, and *The Pelican* in three. In the single year, 1937, he was responsible for three epoch-making productions: of *To Damascus, The Saga of the Folkungs* and *The Dance of Death*. The expressive spectacle of the second of these overwhelmed its audiences, but more typical was the centring of his flexible and imaginative staging in an acting performance of great psychological strength: the long experience of Lars Hanson in Strindberg's leading roles made him the Strindberg actor *par excellence*. Molander's 1935 production of *A Dream Play*, which identified the three principal male characters with aspects of Strindberg himself, and his 1942 presentation of *Ghost Sonata* in a setting which reproduced the appearance of a Stockholm apartment house where the dramatist himself had lived, were extreme examples of the tendency to relate the plays directly to their author. Molander's emphasis on the Christian meaning in the pilgrimage plays was also characteristic.

Alf Sjöberg, best known here for his film of *Miss Julie*, prize-winner at the Cannes film festival of 1951, and Ingmar Bergman both admitted an enormous debt to Molander. Sjöberg directed at Dramaten for forty years and was responsible for two productions, one early, one late, of a number of the plays: *Miss Julie* (1949, 1962), *Erik XIV* (1950, 1977), *Master Olof* (1951, 1972).[13] He had presented *Storm* in 1933 and *Crimes and Crimes*, with Harriet Bosse as Henriette, in 1936, *Charles XII* in 1940, an interesting conflation of *Playing with Fire* with *The Dance of Death* under the title *Fire and Water* (*Elden och Vattnet*), in 1969, *The Burned House* in 1970 and *Strindberg's Margit* (*Sir Bengt's Wife*), in 1971. The list is notable for the absence of the more mystical plays. In addition to *Miss Julie*, Sjöberg was responsible for well-liked film versions of *The Father* (1968) and *Erik XIV*, this last under the title *Karin Månsdðtter* (1954) which, allowing for the freedom of the different medium, still give a fair idea of his general view of Strindberg's work.

Ingmar Bergman's principal stage productions of Strindberg[14] were given while he was director of the Malmö City Theatre in the 1950s (*The Crown Bride* in 1952, *Erik XIV* and *Ghost Sonata* in 1954) and at Dramaten (*A Dream Play* as a chamber play, first in the studio theatre, then on the main stage, in 1970; another production of *Ghost Sonata* in 1973 and an exciting version of *To Damascus* I and II in 1974 which departed from Molander's identification of the Unknown with Strindberg to make him an ordinary representative human being, realistically portrayed). In addition, he has directed some eight of the plays for Swedish radio and television. He has declared a particular interest in the form of the chamber play, and his first attempt on *Ghost Sonata* was in a student production of 1941. Although his adaptation of *A Dream Play* tends to secularise the work, his 1954 version of *Ghost Sonata* showed a progress towards atonement and treated Hummel as a figure of some tragic quality. His 1973 production emphasised disillusionment, and the process of stripping away falsehood was most forcefully realised in the episode where the Colonel's pretences are exposed, when Bergman had the figure (played by Anders Ek) on his knees before Hummel, taking off his uniform, his wig and even removing his false teeth. In general, Bergman's Strindberg productions have been marked by austerity in the staging, doing away with everything which might distract from the acting performances, but also realising the fluid 'musical' structure.

Finally, Lennart Hjulström's staging of a number of the history plays (*Master Olof, Gustav III* and *Gustav Vasa*) at Göteberg in 1969, 1974 and 1975, claims a mention for the revelation of Strindberg as a political dramatist of the first order and of considerable modern relevance. When his *Gustav III* was seen at the Edinburgh Festival in 1974, the critics were unprepared and unable to make much of the performance, but a letter in *The Guardian* (16 September 1974) referred to the play as 'a major commentary on the nature of power and revolution superbly performed . . . comparable in stature to "Danton's Death" ' and pointed out that the whole range of Strindberg's historical drama was still unknown to 'our own classic stage'.

Appendix

Note on Frida Strindberg's Return to England

Frida Uhl was an admirably strong-minded woman, in love with the arts and the colourfulness of bohemian life. She had a steam-rolling determination to further Strindberg's career. Her subsequent lovers, among them Augustus John and Wyndham Lewis, considerably tougher than Strindberg, showed a tendency to profit from her generosity and then run from her in mock terror and without the contrition her suicide attempts perhaps sought. From June 1912 to February 1914 she gave London its first continental-style cabaret, nightclub and associated intimate theatre (which advertised short plays by Strindberg among its other entertainments), called the Cave of the Golden Calf, situated at 9 Heddon Street, off Regent Street. She had commissioned the superb gaudy setting – gilded calf, murals and smaller decorations – from a group of avant-garde artists, including Eric Gill, Wyndham Lewis and Spencer Gore, and various well-known men-of-letters were

also involved. She is vividly conjured up, in her exotic setting, by Michael Holroyd in his biography of Augustus John, 'wrapped in a fur coat, her face chalk white, her hair wonderfully dark, her eyes blazing with fatigue and laughter'. Expensive and fashionable as the place was, offering itself as a refuge for those who preferred to live by night, it was also the meeting place for impoverished young artists (nicknamed 'the troglodytes'), whose presence was doubtless one of its attractions for the rest. Ezra Pound reported how Frida would invite them to her table where the food was free. She had explained to him that it was her need of money which had caused her to take up prostitution 'in this particular form', and he has left a dramatic glimpse of her dismissing one customer from her table with the flamboyant declaration that 'sleep with him she would, but talk to him never: "One must draw the line somewhere".' (See Noel Stock, *The Life of Ezra Pound*, 1970, pp. 144–5, which quotes an account sent by Pound to his mother). Designs for the décor of the cabaret and a letter from Frida to Spencer Gore were included in the exhibition, 'The Omega Workshops', at the Anthony d'Offay Gallery in Spring, 1984.
(See Richard Cork, 'The Cave of the Golden Calf', *Artforum*, December 1982, pp. 56–68.)

Notes and References

1. Biographical: Fact and Fiction

1. See particularly L. Senelick, 'Strindberg, Antoine and Lugné-Poë, a study in cross-purposes', *Modern Drama* XV (1973).

2. For English readers, Elizabeth Sprigge's very readable but derivative biography, *The Strange Life of August Strindberg* (London: Hamish Hamilton, 1949) is likely to be superseded by Michael Meyer's, due to be published 1985. In Swedish, Olof Lagercrantz, *August Strindberg* (Stockholm: Wahlstrom och Widstrand, 1979) has largely replaced Eric Hedén's biography.

3. In 'The Reward of Virtue', *Getting Married*, trans. M. Sandbach (London, Melbourne, New York: Quartet Books, 1977) p. 71.

4. The title of Ellie Schleussner's translation from German, *The Confession of a Fool*, has been abandoned as inaccurate and misleading.

5. Frederick Delius, 'Recollections of Strindberg', *The Sackbut* (London), I, no. 8 (December 1920), pp. 353–4.

6. U. M. I. Dittmann, *Eros and Psyche: Strindberg and Munch in the 1890s* (Epping: Bowker, 1982).

7. 'Sensations détraquées', *Le Figaro littéraire*, 11 November 1894, 26 January and 9 February 1895.

8. Martin Lamm, *August Strindberg* (New York: Blom, 1971), p. 316, 'The Quarantine Master's Second Tale' is included in the collection, *Fairhaven and Foulstrand* (New York: Haskell House, 1972).

9. Title of an anecdotal essay written by Strindberg in 1887; discussed by Lamm, *August Strindberg*, pp. 201–2.

10. *Tschandala*, written 1888, included by Strindberg in third edition of *Swedish Destinies and Adventures*, 1904. Available in French, but not English.

11. *Samlade Skrifter*, ed. J. Landquist (Stockholm: Bonnier, 1912–20), LV.

12. G. Brandell, *Strindberg in Inferno* (Cambridge, Mass.: Harvard University Press, 1974).

13. Eric O. Johannesson, *The Novels of August Strindberg* (Berkeley and Los Angeles: California University Press, 1968).

14. In two vols., 1878–9. See Torsten Eklund, 'Strindbergs verksamhet som publicist 1869–80', *Samlaren* (1930).

2. Naturalistic Plays

1. Trans. Walter Johnson, *Tulane Drama Review* XIII (1968), pp. 113–18.

2. Strindberg's three collections of poetry are: *Dikter* (*Poems*) (1883); *Sömngångarnatter* (1884) trans. A. Paulson, *Sleepwalking Nights* (New York: Law-Arts Publishers, 1978); and *Ordalek och småkonst* (*Word-play and minor art*), included in *Fairhaven and Foulstrand* (1902).

3. Author's Preface to *Miss Julie* in Strindberg, *The Plays* I, trans. M. Meyer (London: Secker & Warburg, 1964), pp. 111, 112. The Preface was written in 1888.

4. First published March, 1889. Trans. B. G. Madsen in *Playwrights on Playwriting*, ed. Toby Cole (New York: Hill & Wang, 1961), pp. 15–22.

5. At Casino Theatre, Copenhagen, 1887.

6. Anna Hoffman-Uddgren filmed first *Miss Julie*, then *The Father* in 1911, with actors from Strindberg's Intimate Theatre. *Miss Julie* is lost. Rune Waldekranz, 'Strindberg and the Silent Cinema', in *Essays on Strindberg*, ed. C. R. Smedmark (Stockholm: Strindberg Society, 1966) sets this in context.

7. [*Open*] *Letters to the Intimate Theatre*, trans. Walter Johnson (London: Peter Owen, 1967), p. 138. Subsequently referred to as LIT.

8. See 'Des arts nouveaux! ou le hasard dans la production artistique', *Révue des Révues*, 15 November 1894; reprinted in *Strindbergs Måleri*, ed. T. M. Schmidt (Malmö: Allhems Förlag, 1972), subsequently referred to as SM.

9. See A. Swerling, *Strindberg's Impact in France 1920–60* (Cambridge: Trinity Lane Press, 1971), pp. 187–8.

3. Out of Inferno

1. Evert Sprinchorn, *Strindberg as Dramatist* (Yale University Press, 1982).

2. LIT, p. 101.

4. In a Higher Court

1. E. Björkman's translation uses the longer, in English more idiomatic form of the title. Later versions attempt to catch the balance of Strindberg's *Brott och brott*.

2. *Strindberg as Dramatist*, p. 240; see whole chapter, 'Making Music', pp. 218–45.

3. See F. J. Marker, *Hans Christian Andersen and the Romantic Theatre* (Toronto, 1971).

4. G. Uddgren, *Strindberg the Man* (Boston: Four Seas Co., 1920), p. 84, mentions Strindberg's association of *Advent* with the English medieval mystery plays.

5. See E. Björkman's translation of *Advent* in his *Plays* by Strindberg, 3rd series (London: Duckworth, 1922).

5. Dramatist as Director

1. *In the Clinic* is reproduced in Göran Söderström, *Strindberg och bildkonsten* (*Strindberg and pictorial art*) (Stockholm: Forum, 1972) and the Munch portrait in SM, facing p. 148.

2. *The Red Room*, trans. E. Sprigge (London: Dent, Everyman Library, 1967), p. 58.

3. Notes on symbolic meanings Strindberg gave to his paintings are given in H. G. Carlson, *Strindberg and the Poetry of Myth* (Berkeley: University of California Press, 1982), pp. 8–9.

4. See J. Casson and T. G. Rosenthal, SM, pp. 14–15, 16.
5. Claes Lundin och August Strindberg, *Gamla Stockholm* (1880–82), (Stockholm: Gidlung, 1974), p. 34.
6. LIT, p. 294.
7. Per Hemmingsson, *August Strindberg som fotograf* (*August Strindberg as photographer*) (Stockholm: Bonnier, 1963) deals most fully with this topic.
8. Passage incorporated in LIT, pp. 81–2; the comparison is extended to the actor's art, LIT p. 127.
9. See especially Birgitta Steene, *Ingmar Bergman* (New York: Twayne, 1968).
10. *Fem År med Strindberg* (Stockholm: Wahlström & Widstrand, 1935), *Strindberg och Teater* (Stockholm: Dahlberg, 1918). Emil Schering's German translation of these notes is drawn on in August Strindberg, *Théâtre cruel et théâtre mystique* (Paris: Gallimard, 1964), pp. 143–9. Reminiscences by actors from the Intimate Theatre, together with readings (in which Harriet Bosse is included), were recorded and are available under the label, 'Röster fran Strindbergs teater' (ALB's dokumentätserie Svenska röster 3, 1968, re-issued 1981).
11. W. Johnson, G. M. Bergman and others misreading Falck, refer to two copies of a composite 'Island of the Living and the Dead'. G. Stockenström gets it right in 'The Journey from the Isle of Life to the Isle of Death: The Idea of Reconciliation in *Ghost Sonata*', *Scandinavian Studies* L (1978). See SM, pp. 113, 285.
12. On Strindberg's knowledge of contemporary theatrical innovations and histories of the theatre, see G. M. Bergman, 'Strindberg and the Intima Teatern' (*sic*), *Theatre Research* IX (1976), pp. 14–47, which includes some illustrations from *Fem År med Strindberg*.
13. LIT, p. 23, 29 Phrases quoted in this chapter without further attribution are from LIT.
14. 'Strindberg and the Theater of Tomorrow', in *Seven Plays and an Essay*, trans. T. R. Buckman (Lincoln: University of Nebraska Press, 1966), excerpted in *Strindberg*, ed. Otto Reinert (Englewood Cliffs, N.J.: Prentice-Hall Twentieth-Century Views, 1971), pp. 90–6.

6. History Plays

1. Starting with the late Middle Ages and continuing into the second half of the Eighteenth Century, the cycle consists of: *Earl Birger of Bjälbo* (1908), *Engelbrekt* (1901), *The Saga of the Folkungs* (1899), *The Last of the Knights* (1908), *The Regent* (1908), *Master Olof* (1871–8), *Gustav Vasa* (1899), *Erik XIV* (1899), *Gustav Adolf* (1900), *Kristina* (1901), *Charles XII* (1901), and *Gustav III* (1902). Michael Meyer has recently translated *Master Olof* and *Gustav Vasa* for BBC Radio.

2. English trans. by A. Swerling (unpublished).

3. G. M. Bergman, 'Strindberg and the Intima Teatern'.

4. LIT, pp. 71, 75.

5. See Gunnar Ollén, *Strindbergs Dramatik* (Stockholm: Sveriges Radios Förlag, 4th edn 1982), pp. 46–8, and plates, pp. 27, 45.

6. See opening of Preface to *Miss Julie* on theatre as Biblia pauperum.

7. At Munich Kammerspiel, 1963 (*Strindberg's Dramatik*, p. 307).

7. 'The Dance of Death'

1. Including Erich von Stroheim, in a remarkable film of 1948.

2. Sprinchorn, *Strindberg as Dramatist*, discusses *The Dance of Death* as conversion drama.

8. Towards Total Theatre

1. M. Lamm, *August Strindberg*, p. 383, quoting Falck, *Fem År med Strindberg*, p. 222.

2. *Sibelius* (London: Dent; New York: Farrar, Straus and Giroux, 1965), p. 96. Strindberg's *Swanwhite*, with Sibelius's music, was broadcast by the BBC, 1949.

3. Strindberg's essay on *Macbeth* is included in LIT, pp. 167–81.

4. Ingmar Bergman's Malmö production is described by Henrik Sjögren, *Stage and Society in Sweden* (Stockholm: The Swedish Institute, 1979), pp. 48–9. Eric Bentley, *In Search of Theatre* (New York: Atheneum ed., 1975), pp. 139–43, reprinted

in *Strindberg*, ed. Reinert, pp. 102–4, praises highly Berthold Viertel's Vienna production of *The Crown Bride.*

5. Title used by Malcolm Williamson for his chamber opera, first performed 1968.

6. Strindberg's essay on *Faust* is included in LIT, pp. 279–89.

7. At the end, the bud bursts into flame, resembling the flowering fireworks over a palace in a famous scene painting for Gustav III's play, *Queen Christina*.

8. See Raymond Jarvi, 'Ett drömspel: a symphony for the stage', *Scandinavian Studies* XLIV (1972), pp. 28–42, and R. B. Vowles, 'Strindberg and Beethoven' in *Växelverken mellan skönlitteraturen och andra konstarter*, ed. G. Svanfeldt (Uppsala: Student Service, 1967), pp. 163–82.

9. It translates a *leitmotif* in Maeterlinck's *L'Intruse.*

10. SM, plates facing p. 126, 188, and plates 30, 40, 42, following p. 215.

9. The Chamber Plays

1. LIT, p. 19; cf. letter to Adolf Paul, 6 January 1907.

2. Literally, *The Burnt Site*, both words suggesting devastation. Sprinchorn, *Strindberg as Dramatist*, p. 260 refers to the Buddhist 'Parable of the Burning House'.

3. A. Artaud, *Collected Works* (London: Calder & Boyars, 1971), pp. 97–105.

4. Dramaten, 1973. See Richard Bark, *Strindbergsdrömspelteknik – i dramer och teater* (Lund: Student Literature, 1971).

10. Strindberg and the Theatre

1. A. A. Grein (Michael Orme), *J. T. Grein* (London: John Murray, 1936), pp. 127–9, 131, supplements information in Frida Strindberg, *Marriage with Genius* (London: Cape, 1937) and Uddgren, *Strindberg the Man*, p. 62.

2. For more complete accounts, see Margery M. Morgan, 'Strindberg in England: A Checklist of Productions', *Theatre Notebook* xvii (1962), pp. 79–83 and E. H. Rapp, 'Strindberg's Reception in England and America', *Scandinavian Studies* XXIII (1951), pp. 1–22, 49–59, 109–37. Gunnar Ollén, *Strindbergs Dramatik* (Stockholm: Sveriges Radios Förlag, 4th edn., 1982) is

the main source of information on Strindberg productions worldwide.

3. *Theatre Notebook*, XVII, p. 144.

4. Winifred Loraine, *Robert Loraine* (London: Collins, 1938), p. 326.

5. *ibid.*, p. 323.

6. Material from interviews recorded by Peter Cotes.

7. *Sex Wars* (Boston and London: Marion Boyars, 1982), p. (7).

8. Only a performance at the Grafton Theatre, 2 April 1936, with Natalie Moya and Donald Wolfit.

9. Notable exceptions: *The Great Highway*, Watergate Theatre, 1950; *Lucky Peter's Travels*, Stephen Joseph's Studio Theatre, 1957.

10. Appendix III to Oliver Sayler (ed.), *Max Reinhardt and his Theatre* (1924) (reissued New York: Blom, 1968), p. 325.

11. The fullest account of Vahtangov's work is given in Boris Zakhava, *Evguéni Vahtangov et son École* (Moscow: Aurora, 1973); a photograph of M. Chekhov as Erik is included with the account in Marc Slonim, *Russian Theatre* (London: Methuen, 1963), pp. 267–8.

12. F. and L.-L. Marker, *The Scandinavian Theatre* (Oxford: Blackwell, 1975), pp. 213–17.

13. Alf Sjöberg, *Teater som Besvärjelse*, ed. S. R. Ek et al. Dramatens skriftserie no. 4 (Stockholm: Norstedt, 1982).

14. See particularly E. Törnqvist, 'Ingmar Bergman directs Strindberg's *Ghost Sonata*', *Theatre Quarterly III* (1973), pp. 3–14, and Steene, *Ingmar Bergman*.

Select Bibliography

Principal Swedish Collections

Samlade skrifter, ed. J. Landquist, (Stockholm: Bonnier, 1912–20), 55 vols.

Skrifter, ed. Gunnar Brandell, (Stockholm: Bonnier, 1945, 46), 14 vols.

Brev, ed. Torsten Eklund, (Stockholm: Bonnier, 1948–).

Dramer, ed. Carl Reinhold Smedmark, (Stockholm: Bonnier, 1962–).

Principal Play Collections in English

1. *Plays*, authorised translation by Edwin Björkman, (New York: Charles Scribner's Sons/ London: Duckworth, 1912–13). 4 series (18 plays, excluding *The Father, To Damascus* and most of the histories). This collection, together with N. Erichsen's (1899) translation of *The Father*, was the source of *Eight Famous Plays* (London: Duckworth, 1949).
2. Edition of the Anglo-Swedish Literary Foundation (London: Jonathan Cape, 1929–39), 4 vols by various translators: *Easter and Other Plays* (including *The Dance of Death, The Ghost Sonata, A Dream Play*), *Lucky Peter's Travels and Other Plays*

(including *The Father*, *Lady Julia*, *Playing with Fire*, *The Bond*), *Master Olof and Other Plays* (including *Gustav Vasa, Erik XIV, The Saga of the Folkungs*), *To Damascus* (new edition New York: Grove Press, 1960).

3. *Six Plays* and *Five Plays*, translation E. Sprigge (Garden City, N.Y.: Doubleday Anchor Books, 1955 and 1960 respectively). Published together as *Twelve Plays*, (London: Constable, 1963), including *The Father, Miss Julie, The Stronger, Easter, A Dream Play, The Ghost Sonata; Creditors, Crime and Crime, The Dance of Death* I & II, *Swanwhite, The Great Highway*.
4. *The Plays*, translation Michael Meyer, (London: Secker & Warburg/ New York, Random House, vol. I, 1964, vol. II, 1975), including *The Father, Miss Julie, Creditors, The Stronger, Playing with Fire, Erik the Fourteenth, Storm*, *The Ghost Sonata; To Damascus, Easter, The Dance of Death, The Virgin Bride, A Dream Play*). A selection *Plays* (London: Eyre-Methuen for the Open University) – *The Father, Miss Julie, Ghost Sonata*.
5. The Washington Strindberg, translation Walter Johnson, (Seattle: University of Washington Press): *Queen Christina, Charles XII, Gustav III*, 1955; *The Last of the Knights, The Regent, Earl Birger of Bjälbo*, 1956; *Gustav Adolf*, 1957; *The Vasa Trilogy: Master Olof, Gustav Vasa, Erik XIV*, 1959; *The Saga of the Folkungs, Engelbrekt*, 1959; *Pre-Inferno Plays*, 1970; *Dramas of Testimony: Dance of Death, Advent, Easter, There Are Crimes and Crimes*, 1976; *Plays of Confession and Therapy: To Damascus I–III*, 1979; *Apologia and Two Folk Plays: The Great Highway, Crownbride, Swanwhite*, 1981; *Plays from the Cynical Life* (one-act plays), 1983. Supplemented by *The Chamber Plays*, translation Evert Sprinchorn and Seabury Quinn Jr., (New York: Dutton, 1962).

Additional plays are included in:

Eight Expressionist Plays, translation Arvid Paulson, (Toronto: Bantam Books, 1965), including *The Keys to Heaven*, with *Lucky Per's Journey, The Great Highway* and better known works.

The Strindberg Reader, translation and ed. A. Paulson, (New York: Phaedra, 1968), including *The Black Glove*.

One-Act Plays, translation A. Paulson, (New York: Washington Square Press, 1969), including *Mother-Love, The Outlaw, In the Face of Death, The Pelican*, with 9 others.

August Strindberg

World Historical Plays, translation A. Paulson, (New York: Twayne, 1970), including *The Nightingale of Wittenberg, Through Deserts to Ancestral Lands, Hellas, The Lamb and the Beast*.

The Isle of the Dead, see R. B. Vowles, 'August Strindberg: A fragment and a survey', *Modern Drama* V (1962).

Adaptations of Special Interest

Ingmar Bergman, *A Dream Play*, translation M. Meyer, (London: Secker & Warburg, 1973).

F. Dürrenmatt, *Play Strindberg* (based on *The Dance of Death*), translation James Kirkup, (London: Cape, 1972).

C. Marowitz, *The Father,* in *Sex Wars* (Boston and London: Marion Boyars, 1982).

Non-Dramatic Works in Translation

(Only the date of first editions is given when there is a modern reprint.)

Legends (1912), (repr. New York: Haskell House, 1973).

By the Open Sea (*I Havsbandet*), translation Ellie Schleussner (1913), (repr. New York: Haskell House, 1973). Also translated as *On the Seaboard* by E. C. Westegren (1913) (repr. New York: H. Fertig, 1974).

Historical Miniatures, translation Rev. Claud Field (1913), (repr. Freeport, N.Y.: Books for Libraries Press, 1972).

In Midsummer Days and other tales, translation E. Schleussner, (London: H. Latimer, 1913).

Zones of the Spirit (extracts from *En blå Bok*), translation Field (1913), (repr. New York: Haskell House, 1974).

The Martyr of Stockholm, translation Field, (London: Thynne, 1914).

Fairhaven and Foulstrand (1914), (repr. New York: Haskell House, 1972).

The German Lieutenant and other stories, translation Field, (London: T. Werner Laurie, 1915).

Tales (*Sagor*), translation L. J. Potts, (London: Chatto & Windus, Phoenix Library, 1930).

Letters of August Strindberg to Harriet Bosse, translation A. Paulson, (New York and London: Nelson, 1959).

Select Bibliography

The People of Hemsö, translation Elspeth Harvey Schubert, (London: Cape, 1959; repr. Westport, Conn.: Greenwood Press, 1974). (See also *The Scapegoat* below.)

'On Modern Drama and the Modern Theatre', in *Playwrights on Playwriting*, ed. Toby Cole, (New York: Hill & Wang, 1961), pp. 15–22.

Inferno, translation Mary Sandbach (1962) reissued, with *From an Occult Diary* (1965), (Harmondsworth: Penguin Classics, 1979). (See also *Alone* below.)

Tschandala, (French) translation Élie Poulenard, (Paris: Editions Montaigne, 1966).

[*Open*] *Letters to the Intimate Theatre*, translation W. Johnson, (Seattle: University of Washington Press, 1966; London: Peter Owen, 1967).

The Son of a Servant, translation Evert Sprinchorn, (Garden City, N.Y.: Doubleday Anchor Books, 1966).

The Scapegoat in *The Natives of Hemsö and The Scapegoat*, translation A. Paulson, (Toronto: Bantam Books/London: W. H. Allen, 1967; New York: Liveright, 1973).

The Red Room, translation E. Sprigge, (London/New York: Dent – Dutton Everyman Library, 1967).

Alone in *Inferno, Alone and other writings* (including *Jacob Wrestles*), translation E. Sprinchorn, (New York: Doubleday, 1968); also translated as *Days of Loneliness*, by A. Paulson, (New York: Phaedra, 1971).

A Madman's Manifesto, translated from Strindberg's French original by Anthony Swerling, (Cambridge: Trinity Lane Press, 1968; University of Alabama Press, 1971.) Schleussner translation, *Confessions of a Fool* (1900), revised E. Sprinchorn as *A Madman's Defense*, (Garden City, N.Y.: Doubleday Anchor Books, 1967).

Vivisection. Rêverie, postscript C.-G. Bjurström, (Paris: L. Mazenod, 1968).

'Psychic Murder', translation W. Johnson, *Tulane Drama Review* XIII (1968), pp. 113–18.

The Cloister, translation M. Sandbach, (London: Secker & Warburg, 1969).

Getting Married, translation M. Sandbach, (London: Gollancz, 1972; London, Melbourne, New York: Quartet Books, 1977).

Sleepwalking Nights on Wide-Awake Days (poetry), free translation A. Paulson, (New York: Law-Arts Publishers, 1978).

August Strindberg

A useful anthology of Strindberg's theoretical and critical writings: *Théâtre cruel et théâtre mystique*, translation Mlle. Diehl, ed. Maurice Gravier, (Paris: Gallimard, 1964).

General, Biographical and Critical Studies

Stellan Ahlström, *Strindbergs Erövring av Paris*, (Stockholm: Almqvist & Wiksell, 1956). (Contains résumé in French).

Hans Andersson, *Strindberg's Master Olof and Shakespeare*, (New York: Folcroft, 1952).

Richard Bark, *Strindbergs drömspelteknik i dramer och teater*, (Lund, 1981). (Résumé in English).

Walter Berendsohn, *The Oriental Studies of August Strindberg*, translation R. Loewenthal, (Washington: Central Asian Collectanea, 1960).

G. M. Bergman, 'Strindberg and the Intima Teatern', *Theatre Research* IX (1976), pp. 14–47.

Gunnar Brandell, *Strindberg in Inferno*, translation Barry Jacobs, (Cambridge, Mass.: Harvard University Press, 1974).

Joan Bulman, *Strindberg and Shakespeare*, (London: Cape, 1933).

Harry G. Carlson, *Strindberg and the Poetry of Myth*, (Berkeley and Los Angeles: California University Press, 1982).

C. E. W. Dahlström, *Strindberg's Dramatic Expressionism*, (Michigan University Press, 1930). Well known, but largely superseded.

U. M. I. Dittmann, *Eros and Psyche: Strindberg and Munch in the 1890s*, (Research Publications, 1982).

August Falck, *Fem År med Strindberg*, (Stockholm: Wahlström & Widstrand, 1935).

Fanny Falkner, *August Strindberg i Blå Tornet*, (Stockholm: Norstedt & Soner, 1921).

Carl-Olof Gierow, *Documentation – Évocation. Le climat littéraire et théâtral en France des années 1880 et 'Mademoiselle Julie' de Strindberg*, (Acta Universitatis Stockholmensis Uppsala: Almqvist & Wiksell, 1967).

Maurice Gravier, *Strindberg et le théâtre moderne*, (Lyon and Paris).

Alrik Gustafson, *August Strindberg, 1949–1912*, (Stockholm: The Swedish Institute, reprinted from Gustafson, *A History of*

Swedish Literature, Minneapolis: Minnesota University Press, 1961).

Karl Jaspers, *Strindberg and Van Gogh*, translation O. Gurnow and D. Woloshen, (Tucson: University of Arizona Press, 1977).

Eric O. Johannesson, *The Novels of August Strindberg* (Berkeley and Los Angeles: California University Press, 1968).

Walter Johnson, *August Strindberg*, (Boston: Twayne, 1976).

——, *Strindberg and the Historical Drama*, (Seattle: Washington University Press, 1963).

A. Jolivet, *Le Théâtre de Strindberg*, (Paris: Boivin, 1931).

Kela Kvam, *Max Reinhardt og Strindbergs Visionaere Dramatik*, (Copenhagen: Akademisk Forlag, 1974).

Olof Lagercrantz, *August Strindberg*, (Stockholm: Wahlström & Widstrand, 1979); translation A. Hollo (London: Faber, 1984).

——, *Eftertanker om Strindberg*, (Stockholm: Wahlstrom & Widstrand, 1980).

Martin Lamm, *August Strindberg*, translation H. G. Carlson, (New York: Blom, 1971).

——, *Modern Drama*, translation Karin Elliott, (Oxford: Blackwell, 1952).

F. L. Lucas, *Ibsen and Strindberg*, (London: Cassell, 1962). Exemplifies resistance to Strindberg.

Børge G. Madsen, *Strindberg's Naturalistic Theatre. Its Relation to French Naturalism* (1962), (New York: Russell & Russell, 1973).

F. and L.-L. Marker, *The Scandinavian Theatre*, (Oxford, Blackwell, 1975).

Gunnar, Ollén, *August Strindberg*, (New York: Unger, 1972). General.

——, *Strindberg's Dramatik* (1948), (Stockholm: Sveriges Radios Förlag, 1982). 4th, updated edition of reference book on genesis and stage history of the plays.

H. V. E. Palmblad, *Strindberg's Conception of History* (New York: Cornell University Press, 1927).

Esther H. Rapp, 'Strindberg's Reception in England and America', *Scandinavian Studies* XXIII (1951), pp. 1–22, 49–59, 109–37.

Otto Reinert, (ed.) *Strindberg: Critical Essays*. Twentieth Century Views. (Englewood Cliffs, N.J.: Prentice-Hall, 1971).

August Strindberg

Torsten Måtte Schmidt, (ed.) *Strindbergs Måleri*, (Malmö: Allhems Förlag, 1972). Essays by various hands; some items in English, French.

Elizabeth Sprigge, *The Strange Life of August Strindberg*, (London: Hamish Hamilton, 1949). Highly readable; lacking documentation.

Evert Sprinchorn, *Strindberg as Dramatist*, (Yale University Press, 1982).

Birgitte Steene, *The Greatest Fire, (Carbondale and Edwardsville: Southern Illinois University Press*/London and Amsterdam: Feffer & Simons, 1973). 2nd edn entitled *August Strindberg: an Introduction to his Major Works*.

Frida (Uhl) Strindberg, *Marriage with Genius*, ed. F. Whyte, (London: Cape, 1937).

Strindbergssällskapet (Strindberg Society), *Essays on Strindberg*, ed. Carl R. Smedmark, (Stockholm: Beckmans Bokförlag, 1966). Contributors include Raymond Williams, Sprinchorn, Rothwell, Northam, Johnson, *etc*. Excellent.

Strindbergssällskapet, *Strindberg and the Modern Theatre*, (Stockholm, 1973). Contributions in several languages.

——, *Meddelanden* (Newsletter), Stockholm, 1945– .

Strindberg Seminar, *Strindbergs Dramen im Lichte neueren Methodendiskussionen, Beiträge zur Nordischen Philologie* XI, (Basel/Frankfurt-am-Main: Helbing & Lichtenhahn Verlag, 1981). Papers (in German, French and English) from the 1979 International Strindberg Symposium in Zurich. Contributors include Gravier, Brandell, Törnqvist, Carlson, Steene, *etc.*

Anthony Swerling, *Strindberg's Impact in France, 1920–60*, (Cambridge: Trinity Lane Press, 1971).

—— (ed.), *In Quest of Strindberg*, (Cambridge: Trinity Lane Press, 1971). Letters received during preparation of previous book. Correspondents range from Samuel Beckett to Charles Vildrac.

Egil Törnqvist, *Strindbergian Drama*, (Stockholm: Almqvist & Wiksell International/New Jersey: Humanities Press, 1982).

Gustaf Uddgren, *Strindberg the Man*, translation J. A. Uppvall, (Boston: Four Seas, 1920).

Maurice Valency, *The Flower and the Castle*, (London and New York: Macmillan, 1963).

Guy Vogelwieth, *Le Psychothéâtre de Strindberg*, (Paris: Librairie C. Klincksieck, 1972).

Select Bibliography

John Ward, *The Social and Religious Plays of Strindberg*, (London: Athlone Press, 1980).

World Theatre XI (1962). Strindberg number.

Index

For the convenience of English readers, the letters ä, ae, a are listed under a, and ö under o. Titles of plays and other works are listed under the appropriate author's name.

Aeschylus 44
Choephori 135; *Oresteia* 135–6
Afzelius, A. A.: *The Saga Annals of the Swedish People* 93
Albee, Edward: *Who's Afraid of Virginia Woolf?* 45, 111
Aldwych Theatre, London 160
Andersen, Hans Christian 61, 128, 175
Antoine, André 2, 7, 30, 75, 81, 148, 173
Apollo Theatre, London 153
Appia, A. 80
Arena Theatre, Washington 162
Artaud, Antonin 139, 160, 166, 178
Arts Theatre Club, London 153
Ashcroft, Peggy 153
Atkins, Robert 149

Balzac, Honoré de: *Séraphita* 59, 123
Bark, Richard: Strindbergsdrömspelteknik 178
Barker, H. Granville 81
BBC Radio 161, 177
Beckett, Samuel 52, 138
Endgame 45, 138; *Waiting for Godot* 45
Beethoven, Ludwig van 55, 110, 132, 178

Index

Bennett, Jill 154
Bentley, Eric 177
Bergman, G. M.: 'Strindberg and the Intiman Theatre' 176, 177
Bergman, Ingmar 67, 74, 121, 122, 130–1, 145, 160, **169–70**, 176, 177, 179
Fanny and Alexander 67; *The Seventh Seal* 67, 100
Bergner, Elisabeth 162
Berkeley Theatre (New York) 148
Berkoff, Steven 155
Miss Julie versus Expressionism 155
Bernauer, Rudolf 163
Björling, Manda 78
Björkman, Edwin 61, 64, 127, 148, 175
Blin, Roger 166
Boccioni, U. 73
Böcklin, Arnold 77
The Isle of the Dead 68, 77, 145
The Isle of the Living 70, 77
Bond, Edward: *Lear* 117
Bosse, Harriet **12**, 78–9, 169, 176
Brandell, G. *Strindberg in Inferno* 18, 60, 174
Brecht, Bertolt 96, 99, 128
Mother Courage 96
Galileo 99
Breton, André 39
Brook, Peter 159
Buckle, H. T. 94
Buñuel, L.: *Viridiana* 106
Burge, Stuart 161
Calderon de la Barca, Pedro: *La Vida es Sueño* (Life's a Dream) 127
Callow, Simon 160
Campbell, Cheryl 154
Cambridge Festival Theatre 149
Carlson, H. G.: *Strindberg and the Poetry of Myth* 175
Casino Theatre, Copenhagen 174
Cassou, Jean 176
Castegren, Victor 167
Cave of the Golden Calf 171–2
Charcot, J. M. 127
Chat noir cabaret 72
Chekhov, Anton 82
Chekhov, Michael (Mikhail) 165, 179
Chichester Festival 155
Cilento, Diane 154, 159
Comédie-Française 166
Conrad, Joseph: *Nostromo* 15; *Victory* 15; *Heart of Darkness* 42
Cork, Richard 172
Cotes, Peter 154, **156–8**, 160, 179
Craig, Edward Gordon 80, 89, 144

Dagmar Theatre, Copenhagen 75, 164
Dali, Salvador 164
Dante 46
Divina Commedia 44, 61
Davies, Gwen Frangçon 153
Delius, F. 9, 71, 173

Index

Deutsches Theater (Berlin) 81
Dittmann, U. M. I.: *Eros and Psyche* 173
Dix, Dorothy 152
Dostoievsky, F: *Crime crd Punishment* 48, 129
Dramaten 4 & n., 78, 97, 163, 167, 169
Dresdel, Sonia 154
Duncan, Isadora 89
Düsseldorf Schauspielhaus 167

Edinburgh Festival 130, 154, 170
Ek, Anders 170
Eklund, Torsten 174
Eliasson (Dr) 11, 47
Eliot, T. S. 145
The Family Reunion 145–6
Elliott, Denholm 159
Elliott, Michael 155
Elvey, Maurice 153
English Stage Company 156
Erichsen, N. 148
Euripides 88
Everyman 53
Everyman Theatre 150–3
expressionism 41, 42, 74

Fagan, J. B. 149, 150
Falck, August 12, **76–89**, 132, 167, 168, 176
Fem Àr med Strindberg 76, 176, 177,
Strindberg och Teater 76
Falkner, Fanny 13, 78
Finney, Albert 155
Flygare, Anna 78, 120
Ford, F. M.: *The Good Soldier* 18
Forfar, Ron 160
49th Street Theatre, New York 162
Freud, Sigmund: *Interpretation of Dreams* 127

Gade, Svend 163–4
Gaiété Theatre, Montparnasse 166
Gate Theatre Club, London 151
Gauguin, Paul 10, 69
Gill, Eric 172
Globe Theatre, London 149
Godfrey, Peter 151
Goethe, J. W. von 9
Faust 41, 46, 48, 61, 122, 178
Goldie, Grace Wyndham 156
Gore, Spencer 172
Göteborg theatres 4, 79, 167, 168, 170
Gothard, David 160
Grandinson, Emil 167
Greek tragedy 25, 26, 29
Greenwich Theatre 158
Grein, J. T. 178
Grey, Mary 149
Griffith, D. W.: *Intolerance* 74
Gustav III: *Queen Christina* 178

Hack, Keith 158–9
Hagberg, J. 91
Hansson, Lars 168
Hansson, Ola 10

Index

Hartung, Gustav 164
Hardy, Thomas 33
Haydn, Joseph 55
Hedén, Eric 173
Hegel, G. W. 51
Helpmann, Robert 161
Hemmingsson, Per 176
Herbier, Jean: *La Songe* (adaptation of *A Dream Play*) 130
Hine, Hubert 149
Hitler, Adolf 164
Hjulström, Lennart 170
Hoffman-Uddgren, Anna 74, 174
Holroyd, Michael 172
Homolka, Oscar 164
Hugo, Victor: *Toilers of the Sea* 15

Ibsen, Henrik 30, 90, 147
Brand 3; *A Doll's House* 29; *The Feast at Solhaug* 90; *Ghosts* 25, 75, 163; *Hedda Gabler* 91; *John Gabriel Borkman* 59; *The Lady from the Sea* 43; *The Master Builder* 43; *Peer Gynt* 41, 51, 65; *Rosmersholm* 23; *The Vikings at Helgeland* 90–1; *The Wild Duck* 59
Independent Television 155, 156
l'Initiation 9, 73
Intiman (Strindberg's Intimate Theatre, Stockholm) 4 n., 12–13, 31, **76–89**, 152, 167, 174, 175, 176, 177
Irving, (Sir) Henry 30

Jacobsohn, Siegfried 163
James, Henry: *The Turn of the Screw* 19
Jarvi, Raymond: *Ętt drömspel*: a symphony for the stage' 178
Jeayes, Alan 149
Job, Book of 62–3
Johannessen, E. O.: *The Novels of August Strindberg* 19, 174
John, Augustus 171, 172
Johnson, Walter 83, 84, 103, 109, 162, 174, 175, 176
Joseph, Stephen 154, 179
Joyce, James 125
Portrait of the Artist as a Young Man 17
Juel, Dagny 10

Kaes, Anton 124
Kafka, Franz 19, 44
The Trial 61
Kammerspielhaus, Berlin 81, 132
Kandinsky, Wassily 71
Kavli, Karin 168
Kedrova, Lila 16
Kelly, Grace 162
Kemp, Roger 160
Kierkegaard, Soren 3, 60
' "Guilty?" – "Not Guilty" ' 60
Kupka, Frank 71
Kurfürstendamm, Theater-am-, West Berlin 164

Lagercrantz, Olof: *August Strindberg* 173
Lagerkvist, Pär 89, 176
Lamm, Martin 174, 177
Landquist, J. 17, 174
Lawrence, D. H. 32–3
Lawson, Wilfred **156–8**, 160
Layton, Robert: *Sibelius* 120
Lehmann, Beatrix 157, 158, 161
Leonardo da Vinci 9
Lessing, G. E.: *Nathan the Wise* 96
Lessing Theatre, Berlin 164
Lindberg, August 75
Lindberg, Per 98, 148, 167
Lindfors, Viveca 162
Littmansson, Leopold 71
Loraine, Robert **151–3**, 156, 179
Loraine, Winifred 179
Lorca, F. Garcia 120
Blood Wedding 120
Lorensberg Theatre 167, 168
Losey, Joseph 156
Loti, Pierre: *Le Pêcheur d'Islande* 14–15
Lubitsch, Ernst 150
Lugné-Poë, Aurélien 2, 173
Lundin, Claes 176
Lyric Theatre, Hammersmith 154
Lyubimov, Yuri 129

MacCarthy, Desmond 153–4
Madsen, B. G.: *Strindberg's Naturalistic Theatre* 174
Maeterlinck, Maurice 2, 82, 119, 120, 127, 130
The Betrothal 119; *The Blue Bird* 119; *The Intruder (l'Intruse)* 79, 88, 178; *The Seven Princesses* 138
Malmö City Theatre 169
Manchester Library Theatre 154
Marker, F. J. 175
and L.-L.: *The Scandinavian Theatre* 179
Marlowe, Christopher: *Tamburlaine* 100
Marowitz, Charles 159–60, 178
Marsden, Roy 160
Massey, Raymond 162
Maude, Hilda 153
Maudsley, Henry 16, 127
Maupassant, Guy de: 'Le Horla' 19
McEwan, Geraldine 155
Merchant, Vivien 158–9
Meyer, Michael 23, 25, 27, 28, 114, 116, 122, 123, 161, 173, 174
Meyerhold, V. 164–5, 167
Miller, Joan 154
Mirren, Helen 155
Milton, Ernest 65
Molander, Harald 167
Molander, Olof 161, **168–9**
Morley, Malcolm 150–1
Moscovitch, Maurice 148
Moscow Art Theatre 81
Moya, Natalie 179
Mucha, Alphonse 69
Munch, Edvard 10, 29, 69, 127, 159, 163, 173, 175

National Theatre, London 155

naturalism 2–3, 6, 9, 15–18, **22–3**, 24, 25, 29, **30–40**
Nazimova, Alla 148
Nemirovitch-Danchenko, V. 81
New Theatre, Stockholm 4, 76
Nielsen, Asta 150
Nietzsche, Friedrich 15, 16, 33
The Genealogy of Morals 16
Nolde, Emil 70

Ockrent, Mike 160
Öland, E. and W. 148
Old Vic Theatre, London 65, 149
Oliver, Cordelia 160
Olivier, Laurence (Lord) 155
Ollén, Gunnar 177, 178
O'Neill, Eugene 3, 19, 150
Long Day's Journey into Night 19, 111
Open Space, London 159
Orme, Michael: *J. T. Grein* 178
Oxford Playhouse 149

Page, Geraldine 162
Palme, August 78
Palmstierna (Baron) 149
Parker, Theodore 3
Paul, Adolf 178
Paulson, Arvid 162
Pavilion Theatre, Whitechapel 148
People's Theatre (Folkets Hus), Stockholm 76
Perfall, Karl von 86
Phoenix Theatre, New York 162
Phillips, Robin 155
Piccolo Theatre, Milan 166
Pickwick Papers, The (Charles Dickens) 14
Pinter, Harold 161
Pirandello, Luigi 36
Pitoëff, Georges and Ludmilla 153–4
Pleasance, Donald 161
Poe, Edgar Allan 19, 137
'The Gold Bug' 57; 'The Murders in the Rue Morgue' 57
Pound, Ezra 172
Power, Tyrone 155
Provincetown Players 150
Przybyszewski, Stanislas 10

quart d'heure plays 21, 22, 38
Quilligan, Veronica 159

Rachmaninov, S. 165
Racine, Jean 88
Ranft, Albert 167
Rapp, E. H.: 'Strindberg's Reception in England and America' 178
Redgrave, Michael 147
Redon, Odilon 70
Regis, Julius 74
Reinert, Otto 176, 178
Reinhardt, Max 81, 88, 132, 162–3, 164, 167, 179
Rimbaud, Arthur: *A Season in Hell* 11
Ring, H. A. 92
Robertson, Pax 148, 149
Rosenthal, T. G. 176

Rosmer, Milton 150–53
Rouleau, Raymond 166
Royal Dramatic Theatre, Stockholm *see* Dramaten
Royal Exchange Theatre, Manchester 156
Royal Shakespeare Company (RSC) 155

Sadlers Wells Theatre 164
Sandbach, Mary 72, 173
Sartre, J.-P.: *Huit Clos* 111
Saville, Philip 161
Savoy Theatre, London 152
Scandinavian Experimental Theatre (Strindberg's) 7–8, 75
Scarfe, Gerald 155
Schering, Emil 176
Schildknecht, Maria 168
Schleussner, Ellie 173
Schmidt, T. M. (ed.): *Strindbergs Måleri* 175
Schoenberg, Arnold 53
Schopenhauer, A. 35
Schuh, Oscar Fritz 164
Seabrooke, Elliott 149
Senelick, L.: 'Strindberg, Antoine and Lugné-Poë' 173
Shakespeare, William 51, 60, 86, 90–8, 100, 127, 157
All's Well that Ends Well 60; *Antony and Cleopatra* 95, 96; *Hamlet* 28–9, 91, 92, 97, 98; *King Lear* 117, 158; *Macbeth* 91, 177; *A Midsummer Night's Dream* 91; *Othello* 91; *Richard III* 98; *The Tempest* 98, 127; *Timon of Athens* 51
Shaw, G. B. 82, 89, 148, 150
Arms and the Man 150; *Back to Methuselah* 50; *Heartbreak House* 150; *Man and Superman* 151
Shaw, Glen Byam 149
Shaw, Lucy Carr 148
Shaw, Robert 156
Sibelius, Jean 120, 177
Sjöberg, Alf **169**, 179
Fire and Water (Strindberg adaptation) 169; *Karin Månsdotter* 169; *Miss Julie* (film) 33, 169
Sjögren, Henrik 177
Slonim, Marc: *Russian Theatre* 179
Smedmark, C. R. 174
Smith, Maggie 154
Snell, James 160
Söderström, G. 175
Sprigge, Elizabeth 117, 127, 130, 142, 156, 173, 175
Sprinchorn, Evert 46, 55, 162, 175, 177, 178
Stanislavsky, Konstantin 65
Steene, Birgitte 176, 179
Stevenson, R. L.
Dr Jekyll and Mr Hyde 23, 42
Stewart, Donald Ogden 156
Stock, Nigel 172
Stockenström, G. 176
Strehler, Giorgio 166

Index

Strindberg, Anne-Marie 13
Strindberg, Frida *see* Uhl, Frida.
Strindberg, Greta 5
Strindberg, Hans 5
Strindberg, Harriet, *see* Bosse, Harriet
Strindberg, Johan August
PLAYS: *Abu Casem's Slippers* 80; *Advent* 40, 54, **61–7**, 104, 120, 149, 163, 164, 168, 175; *The Black Glove* 132, 133, **137**, 161, 163; *The Bond* (*The Link*) 21, 75, 78, 79, 162; *The Burned House* (*After the Fire*) 45, 79, 107, 132, **134–5**, 149, 163, 169, 178; *Charles XII* 49, 96, 97, **107–10**, 164, 177; *Comrades* 21, 35, 79; *Creditors* 21, 22, 23, **35–7**, 75, 111, 137, 149, 150, 162, 167; (*There Are*) *Crimes and Crimes* 40, 48, **55–61**, 78, 79, 100, 116, 117, 137, 145, 150, 163, 164, 167, 168, 169, 175; *The Crown Bride* (*Virgin Bride*) 40, 49, 66, 80, 87–8, **119–21**, 163, 169, 178; *The Dance of Death* 40, 70, 78, 79, 85, **111–18**, 139, 150, 151, 152, 153, 155–6, 162, 163, 165, 168, 169, 177; *Debit and Credit* 21, 35, 75, 149; *A Dream Play* 12, 40, 70, 78, 80, 87, 88, 116, 118, 119, **121–30**, 144, 150, 160, 163, 164, 166, 167, 168, 169, 170, 178; *Earl Birger of Bjälbo* 177; *Easter* 40, 54, 55, **57–9**, 78, 79, 84, 86, 117, 139, 148, 149–50; *Engelbrekt* 177; *Erik XIV* 94, 97, **105–6**, 165, 169, 177; *Facing Death* 21, 75, 79; *The Father* 2, 16, 18, **21–30**, 31, 34, 35, 39, 44, 45, 51, 76, 79, 80, 82, 85, 111, 113, 135, 147, 148, 149, 150, 151–3, **156–60**, 162, 163, 164, 169; *The First Warning* 21, 75, 79; *The Flying Dutchman* 167; *The Freethinker* 4; *Ghost Sonata* 36, 64, 68, 79, 86, 87, 98, 131, 132, 133, 135, **137–46**, 149, 150, 153, 161, 163, 166, 168, 169, 170, 179; *The Great Highway* 79, 179; *Gustav Adolf* 74, **96**, 168, 177; *Gustav III* **95**, 170, 177; *Gustav Vasa* **100–5**, 148, 167, 168, 170, 177; *Hellas* (*Socrates*) 74; *In Rome* 4; *The Isle of*

Strindberg, Johan August–*cont.*
PLAYS–*cont.*
the Dead (182); *The Keys of Heaven* (*The Keys of the Kingdom*) 41, 119; *Kristina* (*Queen Christina*) 79, 86–7, 95–6, 97, 177; *The Lamb and the Beast* (*Christ*) 74; *The Last of the Knights* 74, 177; *Lucky Peter's Travels* 5, 41, 119, 179; *Master Olof* 4, 93, 94, **97–9**, 100, 163, 167, 169, 170, 177; *Miss Julie* 2, 6, 7–8, 21, 22, 26, 27, 29, **32–4**, 39, 44, 75, 76, 79, 89, 91, 95, 111, 127, 137, 148, 150, **153–5**, 162, 164, 169, 174, *see also* Preface to *Miss Julie*; *Mother-Love* 21, 76, 136; *The Nightingale of Wittenberg* 74; *The Outlaw* 79, 149; *Pariah* 21, 75, 79, 136, 149; *The Pelican* 79, 85, 132, **135–7**, 163, 167, 168; *Playing with Fire* 21, 35, 79; *The Regent* 74, 177; *The Saga of the Folkungs* 74, 95, **99–100**, 107, 167, 168, 177; *The Secret of the Guild* 5, 7, 9; *Simoon* 21, 22; *Sir Bengt's Wife* 5, 78, 79, **90–1**, 161, 163, 169; *Storm* (*The Thunderstorm*) 78, 79, 132, **134**, 135, 137, 149, 163, 165, 166, 168; *The Stronger* 21, **38**, 75, 79, 149, 162; *Swanwhite* 13, 40, 79–80, 86, **119–20**, 149, 177; *To Damascus* 7, 12, 20, **40–53**, 54, 61, 78, 79, 100, 104, 106, 125, 133–4, 150, 160–1, 167, 168, 169–70; *Through Deserts to Ancestral Lands* (*Moses*) 74; *World-Historical Plays* 74
OTHER WORKS: *Alone* (*Ensam*) 13; 'Des arts nouveaux' 72, 175; *The Author* 16; 'The Battle of Brains' 15; *The Blue Book*(*s*) (*En blå Bok*) 73; *By the Open Sea* (*On the Seaboard – I Havsbandet*') 8, **15**, 20; 'Le ciel et l'oeil' 73; *The Cloister* 14; 'Deranged Sensations' ('Sensations détraquées') 11, 174; *Fairhaven and Foulstrand* 174; *Getting Married* (*Giftas*) 5, 6, 173; *The Gothic Rooms* 14; *He and She* 17; *Inferno* 18–20; 'In the

Strindberg, Johan August–*cont.*
OTHER WORKS–*cont.*
Cemetery' 56; *In the Red Room* 98; *Jacob Wrestles* 47; *Little Studies of Animals and Plants* 9; *The New Kingdom* 6; *Old Stockholm* (with Claes Lundin) 72; 'On Modern Drama and Modern Theatre' 31, 174; 'On Psychic Murder' 23, 174; (*Open*) *Letters to the Intimate Theatre* 25, 72, 82–6, 91–2, 97, 107, 175, 177, 178; *The People of Hemsö* (*Hemsöborna*) 14–15; *Le Plaidoyer d'un Fou* (*The Madman's Defence/Madman's Manifesto*) 6–7, 17–19, 173; Poems 174; Preface to *Miss Julie* 2, 25, **30–2**, 54, 77, 86, 154, 174, 177; 'The Quarantine Master's Second Story' 14; *The Red Room* 5, 175; *The Son of a Servant* 6, 14, 17; *Swedish Destinies and Adventures* 174; *The Swedish People* 93, 106; *Time of Ferment* 16; *Tschandala* 72, 174; 'Världhistoriens Mystik'
Paintings: 55, 68–71, 175
Strindberg Museum 13
Strindberg Society (Strindbergsällsskapet) 174
Strindberg, Karin 5
Strindberg, Kerstin 8
Strindberg, Siri (Wrangel) 5, 7, 12, 38, 47, 75
Stroheim, Erich von 177
Ström, Knut 86, 98, 167, 168
surrealism 39, 166
Svenska Theatre 78–9
Swedenborg, E. 8, 9, 12, 48, 63, 65, 109, 123
Swerling, A. 165, 175, 177
symbolism 2, 9, 44
Synge, J. M. 15

Taine, Auguste 14
Théâtre Alfred Jarry 166
Théâtre de l'Atelier 165
Théâtre de l-Avénue 153
Théâtre Libre 2, 7, 38, 75, 148, 165
Théâtre de l'Oeuvre 2, 165
Torn, Rip 162
Törnqvist, E. 179
Traverse Theatre, Edinburgh 160–1
Troubridge, (Sir) St. Vincent 149
Turleigh, Veronica 149
Turner, J. M. W. 70
Twain, Mark 20

Uddgren, Gustav: *Strindberg the Man* 63, 175, 178
Uhl, Frida 8–9, 10, 11, 47, 66, 147, 171–2, 178

Vahtangov, Evgeni 165, 179
Verlaine, Paul 71
Viertel, Berthold 178
Vilar, Jean 165–6
Villiers de l'Isle Adam, Auguste 46
Vowles, R. B.: 'Strindberg and Beethoven' 178

Wade, Allan 149
Wagner, Richard 88, 124
Waldekranz, R.: 'Strindberg and the Silent Cinema' 174
Wedekind, Frank 8
Wilde, Oscar: *The Picture of Dorian Gray* 42
Williams, Tennessee: *A Streetcar Named Desire* 154
Williamson, Malcolm: *The Growing Castle* 178
Wolfit, Donald 179
Wrangel, (Baron) Carl Gustav 5, 47
Wrangel, Siri *see* Strindberg, Siri
Wrede, Caspar 154

Yeats, W. B. 9

Zakhava, Boris: *Evgeni Vahtangov* 179
Zetterling, Mai 155
Zola, Emile 2, 18, 39, 136
Thérèse Raquin 2